"If you picked up this book, you have psychic gifts. We live i[...] cally trains us to ignore our inner wisdom, which means that most of us go through life feeling vaguely cut off from important parts of ourselves. Lisa Campion is your guide as you restore the connection to your natural powers. Want more flow, insight, and astounding experiences of what's possible in your life? This book will show you how to recover and use your inherent psychic gifts."

—**Jacob Nordby**, author of *The Creative Cure*

"More of an escalator than a stairway to heaven and back, Lisa's humor and grounded approach make this comprehensive guide to the mystical, utterly accessible. Lisa Campion's latest book, *Awakening Your Psychic Ability*, truly lives up to its name. Perhaps her best book to date, this practical guide is packed with everything a psychic, empath, healer, or dreamer needs to unfold a deeper level of their natural gifts, which we all have."

—**Kelly Sullivan Walden**, author of *It's All in Your Dreams* and *A Crisis Is a Terrible Thing to Waste*

"*Awakening Your Psychic Ability* makes psychic development accessible to everyone! Down to earth, thorough, and full of easy-to-practice tools and processes, it'll teach you everything you need to know to connect to your inner guidance and receive intuitive messages for others and yourself."

—**George Lizos**, author of *Protect Your Light* and *Lightworkers Gotta Work*

"*Awakening Your Psychic Ability* is a manual for developing one of the most important skills of the future. The power of intuition is revolutionizing the way we live our lives, and Lisa Campion's book provides a clear, insightful framework for waking up to the extraordinary dimension inside of you."

—**Kim Chestney**, author of *Radical Intuition*, and founder of IntuitionLab

"Not only does this book deliver what its title promises, it provides a deep and soulful wisdom guaranteed to expand the mind and heart of its reader. Lisa does a remarkable job of helping navigate the broad terrain of psychic phenomena in a way that is both grounded and practical, yet still deeply mystical. This book has arrived at the perfect moment for our rapidly awakening world."

—**Kristin Johnston**, author of *Heal the People*

Awakening
Your
Psychic
Ability

A Practical Guide to Develop Your Intuition,
Demystify the Spiritual World, and
Open Your Psychic Senses

Lisa Campion

REVEAL PRESS
AN IMPRINT OF NEW HARBINGER PUBLICATIONS

Publisher's Note

This publication is designed to provide accurate and authoritative information in regard to the subject matter covered. It is sold with the understanding that the publisher is not engaged in rendering psychological, financial, legal, or other professional services. If expert assistance or counseling is needed, the services of a competent professional should be sought.

NEW HARBINGER PUBLICATIONS is a registered trademark of New Harbinger Publications, Inc.

New Harbinger Publications is an employee-owned company.

Copyright © 2023 by Lisa Campion
New Harbinger Publications, Inc.
5674 Shattuck Avenue
Oakland, CA 94609
www.newharbinger.com

Cover design by Sara Christian; Interior art by Ogmios Lieberman; Interior design by Michele Waters-Kermes; Acquired by Jess O'Brien; Edited by Jean Blomquist

Library of Congress Cataloging-in-Publication Data on file

Printed in the United States of America

25   24   23

10   9   8   7   6   5   4   3   2   1   First Printing

Contents

Foreword

Every once in a while, I meet another psychic whom I feel like I have known and worked with forever. Lisa Campion is one of them.

The moment I met Lisa, I knew she was the real deal. It was as if I'd met an old friend, a kindred spirit, and I knew we'd do great things together. Our connection was instantaneous. My guides buzzed around her, high-fiving her guides like they'd planned the whole thing—which, of course, they did!

It's a big thing to be a professional psychic. It's a huge responsibility. Not only must professional psychics have innate talent, they then must devote a good deal of time and energy into developing their skills so they can use them accurately and responsibly. Once they have done that, they become accountable to help the world with what they know.

That's precisely what I understood from these pages: Lisa's writing is an important part of her gift to the world. In this book, her third, she offers the very best of what she has learned through her years as a psychic healer. She has distilled her own journey and everything she's observed from teaching others into practical and down-to-earth advice to help budding psychics as they awaken their ability. And since we're all constantly learning, the ideas and exercises in this book are also invaluable for more developed psychics who are further along the path.

Lisa does all this in a way that really demystifies the idea of psychic impressions. Contrary to popular belief, being psychic simply isn't that weird or "out there"—it's merely the act of sharpening our intuition. When we understand that our intuition speaks to us in an individualized way, it only makes sense to learn to understand the inner workings of our own wisdom. The truth is that everyone is at least a little bit psychic, and we'll each develop our gifts in a slightly different way. That's why the best teachers don't just teach us what to do; they also help us adapt the lessons to our own circumstances and needs, DIY-style. Lisa's insights serve us wherever and whoever we are—whether we are more left-brained or right-brained, whether we're mediums, channelers, or healers.

And all of us—*all* of us—are best able to serve when we are connected with our ethics. Proper psychic development rests on our ethics: setting and maintaining strong boundaries, putting care and compassion for others ahead of our own ego, and delivering our messages responsibly. Yes, it's very exciting to realize you're psychic—and it's even more exciting to have the skill to share your gift in a way that truly benefits the world. Lisa's emphasis on ethics is invaluable for any psychic at any point on the path, because the ego is tricky and often needs to be reminded of its place.

I'm thrilled to find all that and more in this book. It marks itself as a classic in the field of psychic development—a book that will continue to serve its readers for years to come. As I read Lisa's words, I was struck by their authenticity. She has proven herself to be an experienced and proficient psychic, and the sense of humor and lightness she brings to her work have a transformative quality that lifts us up and helps us find the positive in everything. The advice she shares here is grounded and trustworthy. It clearly reflects all of her hard work and dedication to a practice that is in full alignment with and for the greater good.

If your path as a psychic has brought you to Lisa Campion, know that you're in good hands. *Awakening Your Psychic Ability* will give you what you came to get: useful, ethical, creative advice that can help you develop your psychic gifts for yourself and others.

—MaryAnn DiMarco
Author of *Believe, Ask, Act* and *Medium Mentor*

Heighten Your Natural Psychic Abilities

The other day I went to a party and was standing in a group of people that I didn't know very well. A young woman sidled up to me and said, "Excuse me. I heard that you are a psychic. I don't mean to bother you on your time off, but I really need help. I think stuff is happening to me…you know…psychic things."

Her name was Juliette, and she looked upset, nervous, and maybe a little bit excited too, her hand subtly shaking as she held her wineglass. Remembering how difficult some of my own psychic openings were, I invited her to sit down and tell me what was happening.

"Ever since I started opening up to my spiritual path, all these strange things are happening to me. I see things moving out of the corner of my eye, and when I turn to look, nothing is there, but I'm sure a ghost or a spirit is in my house. I can just feel it," Juliette told me. Then she whispered, "I think I am sensing angels when I meditate, and I see fairies in my garden too." She looked around nervously, as if the men in white jackets might appear out of nowhere to take her away.

"I know things before they happen, I don't know how I know, I just do. And sometimes, I dream things that later come true. Also, my emotional sensitivity is off the charts, and I just realized that I am an empath. I feel everyone else's feelings and have a hard time knowing what feelings are mine. I feel overwhelmed and a little scared at times, although it's also exciting. It would be more exciting if I felt like I had a handle on it all and knew more about it. I keep trying to shut it all down, as I did in the past, but the genie is out of the bottle now."

I hastened to reassure her that all her experiences were very normal and to be celebrated. What she needed was some training so that she could understand, manage, and polish up her psychic gifts. Juliette's psychic experiences commenced when she began doing regular yoga classes that included a daily meditation practice. And, having an interest in becoming an energy healer, she took Reiki classes too.

In our modern life, yoga, meditation, and Reiki are the trifecta of activities that spark open our inherent psychic abilities. Juliette shared with me that she had been very intuitive, sensitive, and psychic as a child: "I used to see orbs of light and other spirits at night, and I would have long conversations out loud with my grandmother who passed away when I was two years old."

However, her experiences upset and frightened her conservative religious family. Because of that, she made a conscious decision to shut everything down so that she could fit in with her family, at school with her peers, and at church.

"I remember," Juliette continued, "being in church when I was really young and asking God to take away my gifts so I could be normal. And it worked. I stopped having those kinds of experiences." At least until she picked up her spiritual journey again in her midtwenties and her natural psychic and empathic abilities kicked back in.

I invited Juliette to join my psychic development program so that she could both understand and develop her psychic abilities. I believe that we have these gifts for a reason and that they are part of our life purpose. They are meant to be developed and used to help us in whatever we are doing in the world. Juliette is a teacher in a nursery school and an artist, as well as being an avid gardener. She worked diligently in the psychic training program and as she developed her gifts, she found that her psychic senses and empathy were an amazing tool to assist her with understanding what her very young students needed every day.

And as she opened up her intuition, her creative talent bloomed. Doing her artwork connected her even more deeply to her inner guidance, since there is a powerful connection between our intuition and our creative process. Her love of nature opened her to working with the spirits of nature, which turned out to be her most intimate and helpful spirit guides.

After Juliette embarked on the same training that you are about to experience in this book, she was able to manage her energy so that she felt grounded, safe, and protected from other people and whatever spiritual energies she might encounter along the way. She is now living in the fullness of her gifts and is excited about how they assist her—not only with helping other people, but also by connecting her to guidance about her own life.

My Story

I could definitely understand and sympathize with Juliette's journey, since it was so similar to my own. A big part of the reason that I teach psychic development to people like Juliette, and why I wanted to write this book for you, is that when I was going through my own psychic opening, these kinds of resources just didn't exist.

I was born into a world where seeing angels and talking to dead people would land you a psychiatric facility. I was definitely one of those "I see dead people" kids. I grew up in the 1970s and 80s just outside Boston, Massachusetts, and spent most of my childhood trying to figure out what was wrong with me and how to make it stop, while trying to appear normal in public, just like Juliette did.

My very first memories are of a psychic nature, seeing colors around people, animals, and plants as well as experiencing the presence of all manner of spirits. To add to this, I grew up in a rather haunted house, a big Victorian beauty, where I used to wake up with the spirits of dead people standing over my bed, wanting to hang out and talk. It was confusing to me why other people couldn't see the sad, lonely, "gray people" that I did.

My mother chalked it all up to my having an impressive array of invisible friends and a very active imagination. At least my hippy parents were relatively open to my experiences and didn't try to totally shut them down or throw holy water on me, as happened to some of my fellow psychics. I felt lonely, confused, and isolated, however, and I spent a lot of time trying to fit in and hide my gifts, in order to avoid being labeled as crazy and strange.

I hunted through the local libraries for books about psychic experience and how to handle it, especially about how to shut it off. There wasn't much, although I was happy to find *Seth Speaks* by Jane Roberts and the works of Edgar Cayce and Carlos Castaneda.

Most of my early paranormal education came from watching horror movies, since I had a life-changing experience when I saw the movie *Poltergeist*. There is a scene in the movie where the psychic Zelda explains what a ghost is and how they get stuck. I remember sitting in the movie theater with full-body chills as I realized there was such a thing as a professional psychic, and I swore to myself in that moment that I was going to do that. And I latched on to her brief explanation of what ghosts really are, why they get stuck, and how to move them on. I was so relieved that someone actually knew something about what was going on. It sparked a lifetime love of paranormal and horror movies, since I felt so validated by them and appreciative that I was not the only one having those experiences. I received an odd paranormal education by watching these movies and learned some things that actually were true along with other things that were highly entertaining in a Hollywood way but didn't hold any metaphysical truth.

I was very lucky that my hippy parents took me to Transcendental Meditation when I was ten years old, since learning how to meditate at such a young age was formative for me and has been a vital part of my psychic and spiritual development ever since. I actually met the Maharishi, and he told me through his translator that he could see my gifts and that I was going to have a rough childhood, but that I needed to hang on because I was going to help a lot of people as an adult.

When I was in high school, our whole family did something called Silva Mind Control (these days called The Silva Method) where I received more training in meditation techniques as well as heard the term *spirit guides* for the first time. (Spirit guides are the helpful nonphysical beings that are here to assist us in our personal and spiritual growth. They could be angels, our beloved ancestors, or spiritual teachers. We will discuss spirit guides at length in chapter 5.)

At university, I studied martial arts and learned much valuable information about how to move energy in my body and the immense benefits of being grounded, disciplined, and physically strong. It was fantastic counterpoint to the more ethereal work I was doing in my psychic development training. During that time, I also welcomed the dawn of the New Age movement, which brought with it books about shamanism, channeling, and psychic development, as well as teachers on these subjects. I spent a few years working at a fabulous New Age bookstore, and I got some excellent training and mentorship with a shaman and a powerful psychic and channeler.

That was about the time that I started working as a psychic myself. I was nineteen years old and have been doing it ever since. When I first started doing readings for people, I could deliver the message, but had no way to help people through their emotional reactions to the messages that I gave them, so I also trained to be a therapist and added that to my tool kit. And then in 1999, I learned Reiki. At that time, I was starting to see colors and energy around people and also opened up some skills as a medical intuitive. I needed help understanding this new level of psychic perception, and one of my mentors suggested Reiki as a way to understand the human energy field more deeply. I have been practicing and teaching Reiki ever since then.

These days I use a combination of psychic work, Reiki, and spiritual counseling in my sessions, and I have shifted my focus to writing, teaching, and mentoring other healers and psychics. I feel passionately about training psychics, empaths, and healers to fully step into their gifts, since the world needs all the healers it can get right about now. My goal is to help people undergoing psychic openings to have an easier time than I did, since I had to learn it all the hard way.

When I was learning, there was no place to find information or a mentor, or to get help, and I suffered tremendously as a child, feeling like there was something really wrong with me. I am delighted to have become the mentor and teacher that I always wish I had, and this is the book that I yearned to find in the library when I was searching for answers.

Now that you know a little bit more about my story and who I am as both a psychic and a teacher, let's talk about what it really means to be psychic, since there is a lot of myth and misconception about it.

What Is Psychic Ability?

Psychic ability conjures up a lot of different images in people's minds. Chances are good that we have seen portrayals of psychics on TV and in movies that stick in our minds as truth, but they might actually be more of the Hollywood variety.

Psychic ability, despite what the media portray, doesn't have to be some strange, unnatural phenomena given to the poor tortured psychic as a heavy burden to carry. It's not meant to dial you into every haunted house within a twenty-mile radius or to attract shadowy spirits whose motive is to scare the life out of you at 3 a.m. every morning. We don't generally flop around on the floor having fits when we have visions or get stalked by scary paranormal beings wherever we go.

Psychics are not in league with the devil (any more than anyone else could be), and it's not a dark gift that's meant to be used for whatever infernal and nefarious plans the cult master has cooked up.

Having psychic ability is very normal—in fact everyone has some degree of ability. It's like athletic or musical ability; everyone has some natural ability, and while it's true that some people might have more talent than other people, you still need to study and practice to maximize your potential.

It is a gift that is meant to help guide us through our life, to assist us in discovering and walking our life's purpose, and to help us serve other people too. Our psychic awareness connects us to our own inner wisdom and is meant to help us navigate through the uncertain nature of life on planet Earth, and it also directs us toward a more soulful and fulfilling life. Our intuition is part of our instinct for survival as well as a guiding light, moving us more deeply into our life's purpose.

I can pretty much guarantee that at some point in your life, you have had a psychic experience, especially if you are reading this book. The truth is that psychic awareness is so common, ordinary, and useful that it probably happens to you ten times a day. And your life will benefit greatly if you pay attention and further develop these skills.

You have had a psychic experience if you

- have not only known that the phone was about to ring, but also knew who was calling, before it even rang,

- had a dream or even a daydream that came true,

- said to yourself, *I knew that was going to happen* or *I had a bad feeling about that…*,

- are an excellent judge of character and know when people are not being honest,

- heard a little voice in your head that tells you to take your umbrella or pick a different traffic route home, and when you do, you avoid the rain and a traffic jam,

- had a nudge or a hunch that someone you cared about wasn't doing well and needed a call or a visit,

- have been at the right place at the right time to help out a stranger,

- have felt creeped out in a place that you visited and sensed that something bad happened there, or

- have experienced the presence of a loved one that has passed away before you found out that the person was gone.

These are examples of very normal psychic experiences that I heard about from my students just in the past week. The bottom line is that, for the most part, psychic experiences are totally normal and nothing to be afraid of, although we are going to talk soon about how to release any fears that you may have. But first, let's continue by defining some terms.

Defining Psychic Terminology

This is really a matter of personal semantics, but it's important that we are all on the same page for these psychic terms.

Psychic awareness is a broad, umbrella term that I use to define a larger set of skills. The two main parts of psychic awareness are intuition and psychic ability.

Intuition is our inner knowing, our own inner guidance. When we receive an intuitive message, we basically are tapping into our own inner wisdom. This is a powerful and useful gift that is available to all of us, and it's one that grows stronger when we pay attention to it. To put it into more metaphysical terms, intuition is information given to you by your own soul.

Whereas intuition is an "inside job," *psychic ability* allows us to connect with sources of information from outside ourselves. This outside source of information comes from our spirit guides that are working to help us along our path of personal and spiritual evolution.

Spirit guides are benevolent, nonphysical beings that choose to assist us on our journey. In the readings that I have done in the past thirty years—over fifteen thousand of them—I have never encountered a person that didn't have a team of spirit guides. Their job is to protect us, guide us, cheer us on, and to comfort and heal us. It might be your beloved granny who passed away and is still watching over you, or it could be angels or earth spirits around you. Most of us have a team of these beings working with us, and they help us whether we know about them or not.

If spirit guides are helpful spirits, I use the term *entities* to reference nonhelpful spirits. They are relatively rare, but we do sometimes encounter them; we will learn how to effectively handle them in chapter 5. Throughout this book, we will explore all the different types of guides so that, by the end of the book, you will have a good idea about who your team of spirit guides really is.

We receive our intuitive and psychic information through our *psychic senses.* Most people have a range of these senses, which can also grow and develop with the right knowledge and practice. A psychic sense might be hearing a little voice inside your head that gives you extra-useful advice, or having a gut knowing or feeling about things. Most psychics also receive psychic information through their bodies too, and, of course, there is the classic visual psychic who sees things, more like little movies with the inner eye.

You will already have some of your psychic senses open, and this may be where your natural talents lie. And, as I said above, the psychic senses can also be developed and expanded on with practice. We will delve deep into understanding what our unique psychic senses are in chapter 3.

I often refer to people with strong psychic abilities as *sensitives,* but it's a term that I use interchangeably with *psychic.* People might have any combination of psychic abilities, but sensitives tend a little more toward the feeling psychic gifts that we will explore in chapter 3.

Chances are very good that if you are reading this, you have had some kind of psychic opening. This happens in many different ways for people, and your journey and experience are, of course, unique. And yet, there are some common trends and patterns that are worth discussing.

Psychic Openings

A *psychic opening* happens when our psychic abilities kick into gear and our talents makes themselves known. For some people, this happens very quickly, almost overnight, and it is attached to an event in their lives, like the death of someone close to them or powerful personal transformation.

Other people open up a little more slowly over a period of time. The gradual psychic opening is a gentle and easy way to go through this process, and it is akin to gradually turning up the lights slowly over time. In these cases, we have a chance to get used to our psychic gifts as they emerge and integrate them as we go along. Maybe you notice that your dreams are more frequent and more vivid than they were before, or that your intuition is happening all the time and your life is full of synchronicities, signs, and omens that confirm your intuitive hits.

Vivienne described her gradual psychic opening as becoming more and more aware of an interconnected flow of events and awareness that helped lead her forward on her spiritual path: "I get strong feelings about things, and I know things too. It was like a beautiful feedback loop as I paid more attention and acted on this awareness more often, and my life aligned in such beautiful ways. And the more I listened, the more intuitive I became. I felt guided toward a life of more joy and meaning, and over a period of about five years, my life has totally changed. I live from my heart and my gut now, and let my intuition guide me."

Vivienne is a lovely example of how our psychic abilities can open in a gradual and harmonious way for us. Other people have a more sudden psychic opening, which is more like having the light bulb switched on. This can bring with it great illumination and also some challenges.

Sudden Psychic Openings

It can be difficult and scary to have your psychic abilities pop open suddenly and strongly. Called *a sudden psychic opening,* it's like a dam bursting and the resulting flood of psychic experiences can be seriously destabilizing.

I recently worked with a young man named Kyle who was struggling through a sudden psychic opening. He was sensitive as a child, but was managing it until he went to Thailand for a six-month-long immersive yoga teacher training program. "I went from being a college student, studying and partying, to spending six to eight hours a day doing yoga and meditation. I stopped drinking alcohol, ate a vegetarian diet, and within a few weeks, I had a very sudden and powerful spiritual and psychic awakening," Kyle told me.

"One day on the yoga mat, I felt something expand and click open inside my head. I went through a few hours of spiritual ecstasy and bliss, where I was feeling at one with the universe. It was amazing, but it also blew open my psychic abilities so quickly that I fried out my nervous system and blew up my psychic circuits. Suddenly, I felt too open and exposed, like a raw nerve. I could see colors around everything and knew way more about people than I wanted to. And I couldn't shut it off either. I was on the verge of a spiritual, mental, and emotional breakdown."

Kyle's psychic ability opened so quickly that he was not able to turn it off or to integrate what he was experiencing. He had visions that he couldn't turn off and was afraid he was losing his mind. Kyle recognized that his unhealed issues were coming to the surface to be attended to, and he was wise enough to lean into the work and seek healing as he needed it. After working through all the grounding and centering practices—I will teach these to you in chapter 2—and doing his own inner work, he was able to integrate his psychic experiences in a healthy way.

Kyle's experience was extreme. The signs of a sudden psychic opening vary from person to person and depend a lot on what our natural psychic abilities and skills are. For the most part, it includes having our psychic abilities switch on very suddenly, which leaves us feeling overwhelmed, confused about what is happening, and longing for a way to understand it all, and, better yet, turn it off when we need to. Teisha, one of my students, likened it to suddenly having a floodlight illuminate a previously dark room. She began to see the spirits of the dead all around her, and she could hear muttered conversations and a high-pitched ringing in her ears. She knew they were talking to her, but couldn't figure out how to hear the messages clearly. Teisha was also overwhelmed by other people's emotions, as her empathic abilities opened up fully.

Sudden psychic openings can happen as the result of spiritual practice as in Kyle's case, but often they are the result of a dramatic, initiatory experience that shifts and shocks us into a sudden opening. Here some examples of what can precipitate a sudden psychic opening:

- long periods of time doing spiritual practice like meditation or yoga

- a near-death experience or a serious illness that brings us close to death

- the death of a loved one or a powerful loss, such as a breakup or divorce

- sudden and extreme shift in circumstances, like a move, a crisis, or a natural disaster, which is also sometimes a brush with death

- psychedelic drugs like ayahuasca, LSD, DMT, or psilocybin mushrooms

These events can crack us open and create a powerful shift in our consciousness. Any circumstance that provides us with a direct and personal experience of the divine source can open up our psychic and spiritual energy centers in a sudden way that floods us with psychic experiences.

Sudden psychic openings can take a dark and scary turn when they happen to people who have a lot of unprocessed trauma. I met Becky after she attended an ayahuasca retreat and experienced a sudden psychic opening that almost landed her in a psychiatric hospital. Ayahuasca is a powerful psychedelic substance that can lead to beautiful experiences with ourselves and the cosmic consciousness, but in her case, it brought her face to face with some profound traumas that she had endured as a child and hadn't yet truly examined or healed.

When she combined unhealed trauma with the sudden psychic opening that ayahuasca brought her, she suffered a severe emotional and mental breakdown and experienced a few weeks where she couldn't function. The angels that had appeared to assist her in healing seemed like demons to her, and she was briefly lost in pain, depression, and anxiety.

Becky was able to get the help she needed by working with experienced healers, therapists, doctors, and other mental health specialists who helped her begin to acknowledge and heal from her childhood trauma. She also learned to moderate her psychic experiences in a healthy way for her, but she said the sudden psychic opening brought on by her ayahuasca journey was an unpleasant and destabilizing experience. (Plant medicines are very safe and healing when done with care and in a therapeutic setting.) Although many people can navigate a sudden psychic opening and remain stable, in her case, the psychic opening plus her trauma created psychic and emotional turbulence that she had trouble integrating.

If you are in the middle of something like that, don't panic. This is a huge opportunity for personal and spiritual growth for you. The energy management practices that we will cover in chapter 2 will help you ground and center yourself, and also help you to integrate the experiences you are having as well as learn to manage the flow of psychic experiences.

It's vitally important to recognize, acknowledge, and take action if you are feeling unbalanced. In general, psychic and spiritual openings call us to our healing, and it's a powerful opportunity, if we answer that call. I strongly urge you to seek healing if you have trauma that you haven't yet addressed. Our inner healing work needs to go hand in hand with our spiritual and psychic unfoldment, or we run the risk of becoming unbalanced as Becky did. In addition to this, it is very important that you attend to your mental and emotional health along the way and make this your highest priority.

I do not recommend psychic development to people that are in an active mental health crisis.

If your mental health is unsteady at the moment, please take the time to get help and stabilize your mental health before you continue your psychic development. You might greatly benefit from the energy management practices that we learn in chapter 2, and a gentle meditation or yoga practice. But rather than dive deep into psychic development work, it's better to focus your energy on working with mental health professionals that can help you stabilize yourself first. If your psychic opening also brings up past trauma, it's vital for you to acknowledge this and receive help for it. In either case, please seek professional help, get medication if you need it, and also embrace healing work and therapy.

Developing Our Psychic Skills: What You'll Learn in This Book

Now that we have a big-picture view of what our psychic awareness really is, let's discuss what it takes to fully develop your gifts. I have been teaching psychic development programs for over twenty years now, and I have found a method to bring out the best in your psychic awareness.

We need two key practices to fully develop our skills: the right knowledge and a chance to exercise our skills and get feedback. We will cover both of these key practices as we move through this book, which will be a combination of knowledge plus exercises, reflections, and guided meditations that will give you the practical experience you need in conjunction with the knowledge.

Let's quickly review what we will be learning together in this book. We will spend chapter 1 laying out the foundational skills that we need, including learning how to tune in and trust our psychic hits, and how to share our psychic impressions ethically and with integrity.

Once we have the foundation built, we will explore how to work safely and sensibly to develop some practical psychic self-defense. In chapter 3, we will explore the world of your psychic senses and give you lots of techniques to identify and open up your psychic senses.

Once our psychic senses are fully open, we will begin to unlock how dreams, signs, and omens act as signposts along the way. It takes some work to learn to decode the messages inside these psychic experiences, and once we do, we can tap into a rich source of psychic information that can help guide us along the way. Chapter 4 is chock-full of practice exercises and tips to help us access this information. We will also learn how to use divination tools, such as oracle cards, runes, and the I Ching, to help us confirm and expand on our psychic hits.

In chapter 5, we will cover how our guides work with us and what the rules of engagement are. We will explore all the different functions that guides can serve in our lives, whether it be as teachers, healers, or guardians. We will also discover how to work with them, since our relationship with our guides needs cultivating. We will do some fun guided meditation work that will give you an opportunity to meet your guides.

Next, in chapter 6, I will share with you a map of the psychic realms, and then, in the rest of the book (chapters 7–11), we will work our way through the map. I break down the psychic worlds as I experience them into four different *realms,* and we will journey together to explore these realms. This will give you an opportunity to experience with it's like working with different types of guides, including these:

- the inhabitants of the lower realm, including shamanic guides and power animals

- the middle realm with your ancestor spirits, your soul mates, and soul family (here we will talk about what happens when you die and why some people get stuck)

- also, in the middle realm, nature spirits such as fairies, elementals, and the other denizens of the devic realm

- beings of the upper realm, including angels, ascended masters, and other beings of pure consciousness.

Going through the different realms also helps us achieve the psychic skill of *discernment,* which is the ability to tell what kind of spirit you might be encountering. Discernment is a very important psychic skill, and going through the different realms is a powerful and fun way to learn discernment skills. During my own psychic development, I came to see the process as a lot like being street smart. The more we know, the safer and less afraid we are. If you have good common sense and know what you need to know, you can enter this world with confidence and ease. It's really helpful to have a map if you are going to be street smart!

Besides knowing what you need to know, the next critical component of psychic development is practice. Psychic ability is like a muscle, and we need to exercise this muscle. We can know all we need to know, but we still need to find a way to work out that muscle to strengthen and improve it. If you want to be physically fit, eventually you need to put down the books and hit the gym, right? We will be doing the psychic equivalent of that with our psychic exercises. Our psychic "workout" will be a series of guided meditations, journal exercises, and other practices that you can do either solo or with a partner to help you make your psychic ability both practical and applicable to your daily life. Audio recordings of some meditations will be available for download at this book's website: http://www.newharbinger.com/50744. See the very back of this book for details.

The Psychic Journal

I recommend that you record your psychic experiences in a journal as part of this practical work. I encourage you to get a journal that you devote solely to your exploration of your psychic abilities. As we move through the material in this book, I will invite you to use your journal to write down any psychic impressions that you have and to record your dreams, your card pulls, and any signs and omens you notice. (Don't worry—we'll cover all of that in subsequent chapters.)

Psychic hits can have an ephemeral quality to them, and you might have the strongest impression of something that you lose track of a few hours later. If you get the hit on a Monday and something confirms it a few days later, you might have forgotten about it, whereas if you record it in your psychic journal, you will remember it and connect the dots. Whatever we pay attention to and put our time and energy into gets stronger and develops. If you do this, I guarantee you will be amazed at how psychic you already are!

Clearing Fear and Resistance About Our Gifts

I do sometimes work with psychic students who have no fear of their gifts at all. They are wide open and ready to jump into learning with only joy and excitement in their hearts. If that is where you are, wonderful! You will be able to dig right in without any fear and resistance. However, most of my students bring with them some fear about their own psychic abilities that needs to be worked through.

There are generally two types of people who undertake this type of psychic development. First, there are the folks that are having a psychic opening and are overwhelmed by psychic experiences that they can't control or understand. They need help learning to modulate and understand their own experiences. They need help turning it "off."

And, second, there are those who want to open up their psychic abilities even more. They have moments where their psychic abilities are full on and they experience psychic impressions, but then it all shuts down again. Their experiences are frustratingly elusive, and try as they might, they can't seem to have the depth of psychic experiences they desire. They want to turn it all "on."

No matter which camp you are in, you might also have fears that need to be addressed. Maybe you fear that you will see bad things if you open up, or perhaps you did when you were little and chose to shut down your gifts. Or you might be working through religious or cultural messages that say it's not okay to be psychic and that those gifts come from dark sources. Many people have been told that they are crazy for experiencing the spiritual worlds, and they fear that they might actually be mentally ill as they begin to see, hear, and sense things other people don't. Or perhaps you fear that you are not psychic enough and that your experiences aren't special or good enough.

Let's take a look at two of my students. On one hand we have Nina who is overwhelmed with her psychic opening and is trying to control her experiences and find the off switch. And then there's Alexis who is frustrated that she doesn't get psychic hits when she wants them and feels that everyone else is more psychic than she is.

Nina was a highly sensitive and psychic child and, in fact, comes from a long line of psychic healers. Many of her family members, especially the women in her family, had visions of the future and could tell when someone was going to die or a new baby was coming.

"My family is from Mexico, so they are also very Catholic. Everyone was fine with psychic experiences, although no one called it that. It wasn't a big deal, we all just knew things and one of my aunts was a famous local healer, a *curandera.* But I also went to Catholic school and the nuns there weren't so understanding," she told me. There was one incident where Nina was punished for telling the nuns about her psychic experiences, and so she decided to shut down her psychic abilities. At that time, Nina's family also moved to a bigger city and an apartment that was very haunted. It was easier to keep a tight lid on her abilities and shut them all down than to feel the suffering of the people around her and see the spirits of the dead that roamed around her neighborhood.

When she was in her early thirties, a health scare reopened her psychic abilities to full on. Nina experienced a dramatic increase in her natural psychic ability and made the decision to begin her training. "I found that it was interfering with my life since it would switch on with no warning. Once at a party, I was suddenly overwhelmed with psychic information that I couldn't seem to shut off. I would also know way too much about my coworkers, and my psychic abilities would suddenly pop open at inconvenient moments. It felt very intrusive and was way too much information about all the other people in my life," she complained. Nina needed to learn how to turn her abilities off when she was out in public. She benefited greatly from the energy management practices to clear up her energy and set up strong boundaries so that she wasn't flooded and overwhelmed by unwanted psychic information.

Alexis was having issues at the other end of the spectrum. As an engineer, she had a logical and practical turn of mind and never considered herself psychic at all, but she always had a fascination with the topic. She loved books and TV shows that featured paranormal and psychic experiences, and at times, she thought she knew and felt things of a psychic nature. Her fears were about not being good enough. She compared herself to others and felt she lacked the skills she needed. She also dismissed her own real psychic hits as nothing special. Alexis had resigned herself to not being psychic at all, when a visit from a recently departed relative handed her a psychic experience that she couldn't deny.

Alexis was determined to open up her psychic ability and used the techniques that we will be going through in this book to acknowledge that her gifts were indeed there. She needed to drop her expectations that she was going to "see" things. She realized that she had a strong sense of knowing and that her psychic impressions where more practical and grounded than the psychics that she saw on TV.

Alexis told me, "I was completely dismissive of my real psychic abilities, of knowing, feeling, and sensing things, since none of that seemed as special or sexy as the psychics who can see things. My gifts were just so ordinary, and, because I had been experiencing them on a daily basis my whole life, I dismissed them all. I truly thought everyone just knew things. Now I see that my psychic abilities are very strong, reliable, and highly accurate. And best of all, they are really useful in my daily life and in a very practical way. "

In order to be ready to fully open our gifts, it benefits us to examine our fears and our past bad experiences, and to clean up any trauma we have had that being sensitive has brought us. See if any of these resonate with you:

- People will think I am crazy. They put people who see spirits and hear voices in mental hospitals, right?

- I will actually go crazy, since psychic and psychotic differ by only a few letters. I just want to be normal.

- I will perceive bad and scary things that I can't control, and maybe I'll even attract more of them my way. I just don't want to know those things.

- I am not special enough to be psychic. I am just ordinary!

- People will make fun of me and not think it's real. I am going to be shamed and humiliated for my gifts.

- They will think the gifts are evil and from the devil.

These are the most common fears that I hear about, but you might have your own that I didn't list here. In order to examine and release your fears, here is a powerful journal exercise to help you bring some light to your fears.

Exercise: Releasing Fear

To examine and release your fear, I invite you to consider these things and journal about them.

- ✳ What are you the most afraid about when you consider opening up your psychic abilities?

- ✳ Did you have any bad experiences that contribute to your fear?

- ✳ What are the beliefs that you learned from your family and your other communities about people with psychic abilities?

- ✳ What beliefs do the people in your life hold now?

- ✳ What do you need in order to feel safe as you open up psychically?

I want to take a moment to honor and acknowledge your fears, but also the fact that you have taken the steps to get trained by reading this book. For me, the biggest antidote to fear has been knowledge. The more I know, the safer I feel in the psychic worlds. The people that seem the most vulnerable are folks that have a ton of raw talent and little training. The more natural talent that you have, the greater your need for training. Going back to my street smarts analogy, the savvier you are, the safer you are.

Rejecting Your Psychic Messages

Often our fear and resistance can lead to a deep denial of our psychic abilities. We may even deny that psychic abilities are real. Besides fear, the primary reasons we reject and deny our psychic gifts is that we might simply not want to hear what our guidance suggests to us. Sometimes our guidance can be about easy things, designed to smooth the rough edges of life. "Don't forget your lunch" and "Your car keys are in your other bag" are helpful, easy to hear, and won't create a strong emotional reaction in you.

But sometimes our guidance isn't so easy to assimilate. Whether the guidance is from your own soul in the form of intuition or it's coming from your guides, sometimes the messages are big, scary, and hard to hear. Our personal self doesn't always like change; this part of us prefers the safety and familiarity of the comfort zone and the "devil" you're familiar with. Frequently, our psychic messages suggest that we must move out of our comfort zone and into new territory. The message might be that it's time to quit your soul-sucking day job and finally become the artist, healer, or gardener that you were always meant to be. Or perhaps the message is that it's time to leave a relationship that no longer serves you, or to pick up and move across the country or across the world.

One of my psychic students is a young man named Nick. As he went through my psychic development program, it became clear to him that much of his depression came from denying who he really was. Nick was a sensitive but was forcing himself to go through law school, more to fulfill his family's dreams than his own. For months, he received strong messages that he needed to quit law school and do something else, but he resisted and denied this message, since it would truly upset the applecart in his own life and in his relationship with his family.

"The more I shut down the messages and denied my own inner guidance, the more depressed, anxious, and ill I became," he told me. It took significant courage to take his guidance seriously, but then he got a strong message that went something like this: *We know it's hard and scary, but you are at a very important crossroads in your life.* Nick saw a flash of two pathways opening up in front of him. In one, he finished law school but also became crippled with anxiety, depression, and poor health. On the other path, he let it all go and saw himself sitting on the beach somewhere watching a sunset and feeling intense joy.

His guides also told him the second path would be tricky, but that his intuition would get him to the right place at the right time. "I took the chance, left law school, and decided I would try and find myself, so I left the East Coast and moved to California." There was plenty of painful drama that he had to deal with along the way, but once he got to California, he rekindled his childhood love of surfing and eventually ended up in Hawaii working in a surfing school. "There was a moment when I arrived in Hawaii and found myself sitting on that same beach that I saw in my visions and feeling that joy. It was a long and sometimes challenging road to get here, but I wouldn't go back to my old life for anything."

If we are going to open up our psychic abilities, we also need to be prepared to hear what our guidance has to say. I am not recommending acting on every little whim and whimsy that crosses your mind, but I am saying we need to be open to hearing and considering it without automatically denying it just because it's uncomfortable.

PSYCHIC TIP: *Declare That You Are Ready*

If you are ready to take the next step in accepting your psychic ability, write a declaration in your journal—something like this: "I declare that I am ready to fully receive any psychic guidance and at least take it under consideration without rejecting and denying it." Remember you don't need to act on all of that, since we want to stay in balance as we move forward in our lives, but it is good to notice, pay attention, and consider your psychic guidance.

Moving from Denying to Accepting

Now that we have worked toward clearing out the resistance that you may have to your psychic gifts, let's step into fully and consciously accepting them. Hopefully you have cleared out your fears and opened up to at least hearing what the messages are without sticking your fingers in your ears and closing your eyes, psychically speaking. Since you are reading this book, we can take it as a good sign that you are committed to at least exploring the possibility of this. I want to take a moment to honor and acknowledge you for that, since I know it's not easy to do.

In my experience of training hundreds of people to master their psychic abilities, it can come as a huge relief to finally allow ourselves to live authentically and fully be who we are. I believe that we have these gifts for a reason, and it is not to torture us. They are very much a part of our life's purpose. As we fully explore our psychic gifts, we will find out what our strong suits are and that can show us what we are meant to do with the gift. People who train up their psychic abilities might discover a hidden talent for mediumship, or a special connection with the angels or nature spirits along the way. You might already have a good idea of where your psychic talents lie, but you also might be surprised and uncover a hidden and unexpected aptitude.

Best Practices for Awakening Your Psychic Abilities

Here are some tips and best practices to help you get the most out of our time together as you read this book. These tips will help you to optimize your training as well as to open up and maximize your psychic awareness.

❋ Don't compare yourself to others, especially to what you see on TV. Drop your expectations about what you think should be happening and tune in to what is actually happening in the moment.

❋ Change the word "see" to the word "perceive" or "experience," since that opens us up to noticing all our psychic senses.

❋ Spend more time tuning in. If we are busy all the time, we don't have space and time to be receptive. Psychic impressions need an empty space in our consciousness to flow into.

❋ Do the practice exercises. Psychic ability is like a muscle that grows stronger with exercise.

❋ Do your daily energy management practices to keep yourself centered, grounded, cleared, and protected while you are engaged in learning.

❋ Practice good boundaries and ethics about who you share your psychic hits with. Most often it's better to keep them to yourself unless directly asked for your feedback.

What's Next?

Now that we have cleared the path for you in this chapter, in the next chapter we'll lay down the foundation of your psychic skills and learn how good psychic hygiene can help keep you safe and grounded as you open. We will also work through how to make time and space to be receptive to psychic information as well as learn some tangible and practical skills on how to trust that what you are receiving is really a psychic impression.

Chapter 1

Build Foundational Awareness Skills

The initial stage of psychic development can be the trickiest for students. All that natural psychic ability and talent is now opening up, but we still don't have the skills and training needed to control our abilities. We need help in order to work through this patchy, shaky phase of our psychic development. So, let's lay down the foundational skills that all psychics need.

These fundamental skills are so important that they remain significant even for very advanced psychics. We practice these foundational skills—like musicians play scales and do warm-up exercises—so we can continue to fine-tune these essential skills. These foundational skills include learning how to tune in and pay attention to the psychic impressions that we receive.

In this chapter, we'll explore how our brain-wave states help or hinder our psychic experiences as well as learn some concrete ways to determine and trust that we are getting real psychic hits. We also need to learn how to tell the difference between a real psychic hit and the mental static and chatter of our own thoughts.

I am excited to bring these life-changing skills to you. If you feel overwhelmed, frustrated, stuck, or maybe worried that you are crazy, these skills can help you deal with those negative feelings and open up to your psychic abilities. Let's begin with learning how to become receptive enough to really tune in.

Learning to Tune In

One of the first things we must do to open up our psychic abilities is to make time and space to tune in. *Tuning in* is a combination of slowing down our busy minds so that we become receptive to psychic impressions and learning to stop and pay attention to a psychic hit when we do receive it.

For many people, psychic hits happen all the time, all day long, and we basically ignore them. Unless we are tuning in, we might not recognize when they do happen, and so they slide through our awareness without our notice. For the most part, intuitive hits are subtle and connected to our feelings, our gut instincts, and our physical sensations. In order to catch them in the act, we need to tune in to what is happening in our bodies, our emotional states, and our inner sense of knowing.

In chapter 4, we will talk about signs and omens, which are events and synchronicities that happen in the real world that are also part of our guidance. They are the winks from the universe that you are heading in the right direction, but if you are not tuned in, you will miss the possibility that the dragonfly that just landed on your hand might have a significant meaning and is actually a potential communication from your guides.

Tuning in is a habit that we need to learn, and yet we also may need to unlearn the habit of being tuned out. It's so easy to walk through life with blinders on, unaware of our own intuitive nature and immersed in our busy minds. In order to master our psychic development, the blinders need to come off. We need to quiet the inner chattering mind and shift our focus both to our bodies, feelings, and gut knowing as well as to what is happening in the world around us. When we tune in, we both take time to slow down and reconnect with ourselves, and find a neutral, open, and receptive state of being that our psychic experiences can flow into. As the Zen masters say, the cup must be empty so that wisdom can flow into it.

Exercise: Tuning In Meditation

This is a simple and powerful way to tune in to your psychic impressions. You can download an audio recording of this meditation at http://www.newharbinger.com/50744.

1. Sit somewhere quiet and close your eyes.

2. As best as you can, quiet your feelings and thoughts. It can help to focus on your breathing by doing a few long, slow breaths. Try a four-count inhale and four-count exhale to settle your thoughts and feelings.

3. Ask yourself a specific question, or ask something more general, like *What do I need to know right now?*

4. Pay attention to any thoughts, feelings, images, and sensations in your body as you continue the slow breathing.

5. Record anything you perceived in your journal.

We need to make quiet space inside us to tune in, and this ability will get easier, stronger, and more accurate as you practice it regularly. I have many different ways and techniques to help you do this. Let's start with understanding a little bit about how we can dramatically increase our ability to tune in by understanding more of how our brains process and receive psychic information.

Left Brain vs. Right Brain

Most of our psychic information is perceived by our intuitive, emotional, and creative right brain. But to make sense of that information, which often comes in the form of symbols, we must then switch our attention to the analytical, logical left brain. Of course, as fully functioning humans, we need access to both sides of our brain. As psychic students, we need to understand which side we are more naturally attuned to, and how to switch our focus as we need to.

The left hemisphere of the brain is responsible for the more logical and analytical brain functions such as these:

- language and thinking in words

- linear and sequential thinking

- mathematics

- logic and factual data

- analysis

The right hemisphere of the brain manages our creative, emotional, and intuitive experiences and is vital in helping us have psychic experiences. This part of our brain helps us process

- intuition

- creativity and the arts

- emotional states

- imagination

- holistic thinking.

Psychic ability happens mostly on the right side of the brain, so people who are already more wired to be right-brain dominant have the edge on people who are naturally more left-brained.

However, a good psychic needs both sides of their brains working in conjunction and harmony. The left brain is necessary to make sense of the psychic data we experience. This is where we find meaning in our psychic impressions, and we rely on our left brain to help us communicate these experiences to others. The left brain helps us to practice discernment, and it's about as good of a bullshit detector as we will ever get.

If we have too little of the left-brain, analytical processes, we can't understand the meaning of our psychic impressions; they seem like incomprehensible gibberish. On the other hand, too much left-brain analysis leaves us very judgmental, skeptical, and unable to relax into the more right-brained psychic experiences. Here is a good example of how these two types of people—right-brain and left-brain dominant—handle psychic experiences.

Back in the days when I did house clearing for people, I went into a very haunted house owned by a couple with young children. Ellery was a sensitive, and he and his two young children were having all kinds of psychic experiences that they couldn't explain. Doors were slamming shut, and footsteps were heard in the attic. Ellery said he felt as if someone tried to push him down the basement stairs, and he did have a fall down the stairs that bruised and scared him.

On the other hand, some of the experiences were funny and sweet. Missing objects were returned, lights flickered, and the radio would come on for no reason. Ellery saw things out of the corners of his eyes and heard the murmur of voices at night. He was having very classic right-brained psychic experiences but was having trouble making sense of what he was experiencing.

Ellery's wife, Stephanie, was a scientist working in a nearby biomedical lab and was constantly looking for the logical explanation for the haunted phenomenon in the house. She called in an electrician to test the wiring and checked for animals trapped in the attic. When that all proved to be fine, Stephanie did some research on the house and discovered that an elderly couple had owned the house and both had passed away there.

I could perceive a nice elderly gentleman who was still lingering and trying to make the new people in the home feel welcome. He had a helpful and playful demeanor, and liked turning on the lights, the radio, and returning lost objects. The former lady of the house was angry that there were strange people in her house, and she was the one making trouble for the new homeowners.

In this example, you can see how Ellery's right-brained psychic awareness gave him the psychic impressions he was having, and Stephanie's left-brained orientation helped solve the mystery of it all. If you are a left-brained person, don't despair. You can still activate your psychic awareness. For you, it will be a matter of relaxing, not pushing or trying too hard, and learning to lean into your feelings a little more. Try not to compare yourself to others, be overly self-critical, or dismiss your experiences because they don't make "sense." You will benefit from truly relaxing and allowing your perceptions to unfold organically, and you will need to learn to feel your way through it all.

Left-brained people can shut down their psychic senses if they overthink things or start analyzing everything too soon. However, a little healthy skepticism and common sense is also a very useful skill set for psychics. Left-brained people often have a strong affinity for the knowing and hearing psychic senses, which we will fully explore in the next chapter.

If you are a right-brained person, some of the exercises in this book may be a little easier for you. You will, however, also need to balance things out and bring your left brain into play so that you can interpret your psychic experiences and bring sense and meaning to them. Right-brained people will often have more visual psychic experiences and often have a strong feeling sense. They may also be empaths.

Right-brained people have no trouble making intuitive decisions, but they sometimes need to balance these things out with a logical plan that makes practical sense. I have seen very intuitive people shoot themselves in the foot by making snap decisions without thinking them through. "My angels made me do it" was what my friend said when she made a series of risky, impulsive, albeit intuitive decisions that led her to a whole world of trouble. These were all based on real intuitive experiences she had, but she would have benefited from bringing that intuition over into her left brain to formulate a plan that made sense and would actually work in the world.

Our goal is to have the best of both worlds—right and left brain. We want to integrate our intuitive and logical selves so they are in harmony with each other and so that both help us to meet our goals in life.

Exercise: Are You Right-Brained, Left-Brained, or Both?

Use your journal to explore whether or not you have a right- or left-brain dominance by considering these questions:

- ❀ Are you more logical, analytical, and perhaps skeptical? If so, you are probably left-brain dominant. How does this both help and hinder your psychic experience?

- ❀ Are you more creative, intuitive, and emotional? If so, you are probably right-brain dominant. How does this both help and hinder your psychic experience?

- ❀ If you have a dominant side, what do you feel you need to do to bring some balance?

Next up is learning about how our brain-wave states can help us when we need and want to tune in. In this case, learning to consciously shift our brain into the alpha brain wave is the key. Let's take a look at how all that works.

Brain-Wave States

While we are talking about the brain and how it perceives different levels of reality, it's a good time to discuss how our brain-wave states impact our psychic perceptions. Brain waves are the result of electrical activity produced by our brain. These wavelike patterns are created by different types of neurological activity that is associated with different types of consciousness. When a group of neurons sends a burst of electrical pulses to another group of neurons, it creates a wavelike pattern. This brain-wave activity is measured in hertz (Hz), a unit of frequency equal to one cycle per second. We have five natural brain-wave states that our brains cycle through, depending on what we are doing.

HUMAN BRAIN WAVES

GAMMA
Insight - Peak Focus - Expanded Consciousness

32-100 Hz

BETA
Alertness - Concentration - Cognition - Learning

13-32 Hz

ALPHA
Relaxation - Visualization - Creativity - Reflection

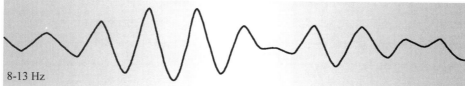

8-13 Hz

THETA
Meditation - Intuition - Memory - Dreams

4-8 Hz

DELTA
Detached Awareness - Deep, Healing Sleep

0.5-4 Hz

|——————————— 1 Second ———————————|

Build Foundational Awareness Skills

Gamma Wave. Gamma is the peak-performance brain wave that happens when we are in deep flow states of consciousness. The different parts of our brains are highly connected to each other in gamma, and we have peak problem-solving, and can access high-level, peak spiritual experiences. We are awake, alert, and in a zone of optimal creative problem-solving. People who meditate and spend a lot of time doing spiritual practices show this brain wave more regularly than those who don't.

Beta Wave. Beta is where we spend most of our waking hours. The beta brain wave is where we do our best thinking; we are alert and engaged in cognition. We're in beta when we are working, learning, and thinking rationally and logically.

Alpha Wave. Alpha is a light trance state, and we easily enter this state of consciousness when we are doing rote and repetitive actions like driving, walking, and washing the dishes, or taking a shower. Also, things like guided meditations and daydreaming create an alpha brain-wave pattern. This is where we are highly creative and intuitive. Alpha is where we want to go to get the best psychic and intuitive experiences.

Theta Wave. In theta, we are deeply relaxed and in a state of deep healing. Certain meditation practices like breath-based, mantra-based, and concentration meditation practices can lead us here too. Most of the time when we are in theta, we are sleeping, but we can get there when we receive healing sessions such as Reiki. If you have ever had a massage or an energy healing session and you had that lovely, floaty feeling of being not exactly asleep but certainly elsewhere, this is what the theta wave feels like. You can't speak or even think clearly—it's deep relaxation and contentment.

Delta Wave. Delta is the slowest brain-wave state, and it's indicative of deep, dreamless sleep. When you are in delta, you have no awareness of yourself—it's lights out. Our bodies go into a state of rest and recharge during this time of deep, dreamless sleep.

✳ ✳ ✳

We naturally go through these brain waves in our sleep cycle. If we want to increase our psychic experiences, we need to increase the time we spend in the alpha brain wave, by doing activities like meditation. When we are in alpha, our psychic awareness is enhanced, our logical and thinking mind is quieted, and we are open both to receiving intuitive hits and messages from our guides and to noticing the signs and omens that surround us.

Professional psychics learn to shift into alpha on demand, and that is part of how they manage to turn their psychic awareness on and off at will. Old school psychics like Edgar Cayce worked in a deep theta brain-wave state, which was called a *trance channel*. This type of psychic would go into a trance that was so deep that they didn't remember what they said when they came out of it. These days there are fewer trance channels around, and most modern-day psychics have learned to make their connection while still being aware of what is happening around them.

When I am working, being in the alpha state allows me to carry on a conversation and do energy work at the same time that I am doing a reading. I work mostly in the alpha state, although if I am going to look at a past life or speak to someone who has passed on, I need to drop into the theta brain-wave state. At that point, I need to sit down and close my eyes for a bit to retrieve the information.

As I mentioned above, when we sleep, our brains naturally cycle through these brain-wave states. It's natural to go through beta, alpha, theta, delta, and then back up again. And we are in gamma when we dream. If you get about eight hours of sleep, you will go through this cycle three or four times. Many people have their most noticeable psychic experiences when they are either falling asleep or waking up as their brains pass naturally through the alpha brain wave.

Rosemary experienced this when she saw the figure of her father standing at the foot of her bed as she was waking up in the morning. "I could see him, clear as day, and hear him as he said my name out loud," she told me. "As soon as I rolled over and turned on the light, he was gone." It wasn't the light that chased him away. Instead, in the act of moving to turn on the light, Rosemary woke up enough to shift brain-wave states from alpha to beta, but in all likelihood, her father was still there.

The Alpha Brain-Wave State

Let's look at some ways to drop into the alpha brain-wave state when we want to tune in. Alpha is a light trance state, where our left brain is quiet and our right brain is more active. Alpha is a light meditative state, and once in it, we are highly creative and connected to our intuition. Alpha happens naturally when we meditate, when we relax and daydream, or when we engage in routine and repetitive tasks. Here are some good ways to get into an alpha state:

•   meditation of all kinds, including guided meditations

- yoga, tai chi, walking, and other forms of repetitive, light exercise where we don't have to think too much

- driving, especially somewhere you have been before, like on your routine commute to work

- doing the dishes, mowing the lawn, pulling weeds in the garden, or folding laundry, anything that keeps the hands and the thinking part of our minds busy

- taking a bath or a shower (Many psychics get their strongest hits in the shower!)

- daydreaming moments such as watching the surf on the beach, watching the clouds go by, gazing into a fire, or just watching the grass grow

To increase your psychic awareness, make a note of what activities put you into the alpha state and make them a regular part of your life. Pay attention to what emerges from your subconscious while you are in alpha. We will often have aha moments that supply solutions to problems, intuitive nudges, and creative inspiration when we are in alpha.

Here is a great example of someone who has learned to cultivate and maximize her time in the alpha brain-wave state. Sureya rides the commuter train for about an hour into Boston every day for work, and she told me that is her best time for alpha activities.

✳ SUREYA'S STORY *Something about the motion of the train and the soothing, regular noise it makes relaxes me and puts me into the alpha state. Everyone else is quiet since I get into the quiet car, always. I bring some work with me, but mostly I think about the things that I need answers to. I write questions, problems, and issues in my journal, and then I let my mind go blank and I look out the window. After a while, ideas and intuitive insights come into my head, and I write those down too. I feel open and relaxed, not pushing but just being receptive and curious.*

PSYCHIC TIP: *Cultivating Your Alpha Moments*

What are your go-to alpha-state moments? Make sure that you spend some regular time doing them. Try this technique. Ask yourself a question, something that you need insight on for yourself or someone else. Write the question down in your journal and then go do your favorite alpha activity. Forget about the question, and just let it cook on the back burner of your subconscious for a while. Be aware of any psychic impressions that float through you—knowings, feelings, physical sensations, or aha moments that come into the empty and receptive space you've created. Note the impressions that you get in your journal so that you don't forget.

We've made some time to listen to our psychic guidance in the alpha brain-wave state. Now let's figure out some ways to trust that the hits that we are getting are real.

Learning to Trust

How do we tell the difference between a real psychic impression and the crazy stuff that we make up in our own heads? This is a tricky and nerve-wracking question even for very advanced psychics, and it can really create a problem for people who are just learning. Our minds can spiral down into doubt so easily, leading us to mistrust and dismiss accurate psychic impressions. Here are some good ways to learn to trust your psychic hits.

The First Impression Is Usually Right—Even If It's Weird

Usually, the very first impression we get is the real psychic hit, as these impressions arise effortlessly into an open and receptive inner space. It happens quickly and effortlessly, almost before you could make yourself think of anything. And then our minds kick in, argue, balk, and we can find ourselves falling down the rabbit hole of doubt. It takes some discipline to learn to pay attention to the very first impression that you have, but doing so will yield powerful and accurate results.

Meeting people for the first time is a great example of this, and one that we can all relate to. I am sure you have had an experience where you met someone and took an instant like or dislike to them. This is our intuitive guidance coming through, and we all know what happens when we don't honor this information. And yet, it's amazing how quickly our minds step in to argue with us and convince us to reject our own inner knowing. If you want to catch the true, raw psychic hit, practice noticing what impressions you have before your mind jumps in.

Drop Your Expectations

Learning to drop your expectations about what you think is going to happen and tuning in to what is actually happening will yield psychic pay dirt. Again, our minds have a tendency to jump in and discard relevant information if it doesn't meet our expectations.

Deirdra, one of my psychic students, was doing an exercise to meet her power animals, and she felt that there was a hummingbird near her. She loves humming-birds, so this was easy for her to believe and accept. The next one she perceived was a snake, but she hates snakes. Here's what she told me.

✳ DEIRDRA'S STORY   *I totally dismissed that hit. I thought it was scary and silly to have a snake as a spirit guide, so I told it to go away and ignored it. That snake showed up in a few more of my meditations and dreams before I relaxed about it and realized that my mind was rejecting the real hit just because it didn't fit my ideas and expectations. That snake has taught me a lot about how to stay grounded and when change is coming for me. It has brought me much wisdom over time, so I am glad I finally listened!*

The real psychic hit is often outside our normal mental frame and by dropping our expectations, we open our mind to view things within a larger frame. Next up is learning to recognize and pay attention to our own bodies for confirmation about a psychic hit.

Learn Your Body's Truth Signal

Every psychic student I have trained has a *truth signal* that they feel in their body. This is your body's way of telling you that you are hearing the truth and getting a real psychic hit. This truth signal is different for everyone, but once we learn to recognize it, we can use it to help us confirm that we are getting a real psychic hit.

It might feel like chills or gooseflesh, or maybe you feel tingly all over. I feel a rush of energy up my spine that starts at my tailbone and goes all the way up to the crown of my head. Sometimes I feel a tingly sensation on the crown of my head too, and this alerts me to the fact that something is going on that I need to pay attention to. My friend Belinda tears up a little when she hears or speaks the truth. She calls these "truth tears," because this is her body's truth signal.

As you go through the practice exercises in this book, pay attention to how your body feels when a real psychic impression arises—you will feel it somewhere. Then you might be alerted to a psychic experience when you feel the truth signal. This is a little easier for people who are naturally grounded and have the body's psychic sense already open, but this can be cultivated even in people who are habitually disconnected from their bodies. This is one of the many reasons why it's so important to be grounded in your body and why our grounding practices, which we will learn in the next chapter, are so vital.

Let's take a look at how to tell the difference between a strong psychic impression and our own fears, anxieties, and other emotional states. It's obviously important to know the difference.

If You Are Triggered, It's Not a Hit

Are you wondering how to tell the difference between a true psychic impression and your own emotions? The simple answer is this: if you feel triggered and emotionally reactive, then what you are experiencing is not a real psychic hit. Real impressions have a curiously detached and nonemotional energy to them, even if you think it's something that you should be emotional about.

When I was in my twenties, I did a semester of college abroad and was living in France. One night, I had a dream about my grandmother. She and I were sitting in a café and chatting about normal, everyday things. She looked radiant and happy, and told me she was just stopping by to say hello and good-bye because she had to leave now. I knew in the dream that it meant she had passed, but I felt only joy in seeing her. It was like knowing a fact and then feeling the sweetness of the moment, but I wasn't very sad or emotional about it all in the dream. I woke to the phone ringing in my apartment. My mother told me that my grandmother was gone, and then I had an avalanche of feelings about it.

One of my psychic students, Martha, is the mother of five children. She is a nurturing but anxious mother, a soft-hearted empath who worries constantly about her brood. She learned to tell the difference between her own anxiety and a real psychic hit in this experience.

✴ MARTHA'S STORY   *One night in the middle of the winter, I awoke suddenly out of a deep sleep. I got up, put on my boots and coat since it was snowing hard, and got in the car. I knew one of my teens needed me, so I drove around the back roads near my house. I wasn't feeling anxious at all; I just had a strong knowing and a pulling sensation in my belly. We live in the middle of nowhere, and there isn't great phone reception at the best of times. I drove around sort of randomly for about twenty minutes, just following my gut until I found one of my teenagers pulled over on the side of the road. His car had broken down, and he was in one of the dead zones for cell service. I know I can be an anxious mother, but that whole time, I felt no anxiety, only this calm sort of knowing that I needed to find him. And I did.*

If you are feeling anxiety, anger, fear, or any other strong emotion, you can pretty much bank on that being your own inner worries rather than a real psychic hit. When we have strong emotions, we lose our own psychic connection, which is why it is easier to read for other people. Even professional psychics have trouble getting accurate psychic information for themselves when they are triggered. This is part of the reason why it's very useful to become adept at using some divination tools, which we will learn to do in chapter 4.

Working with a Pendulum

Another way to learn how to trust our psychic hits is by using a pendulum. Pendulums are great tools for confirming or denying a psychic hit. A *pendulum* is a divination tool that is usually made from a pointed crystal that hangs from a chain or string. They can be made from any material, including brass, copper, or even plastic. You can purchase quite beautiful and elaborate ones in New Age shops, and Etsy has some very beautiful ones. They don't have to be fancy though; a pendulum can be as simple as a safety pin on a piece of string. When I need one and don't have mine handy, I just use whatever necklace I am wearing.

Picking out a pendulum can be fun. Find one that really resonates with you, and tap into your intuition to help you pick one out. I prefer heavier metal ones made from copper or brass, but many people love the ones made from crystals and gemstones. If you are choosing one from a shop, ask that pendulum if it is the right one for you. Here is the best way to work with your pendulum:

Clear and Attune Your Pendulum. Once you get your pendulum, you need to clear any residual energy from it, especially if it's made from crystal. Sage it, put it in a bowl of salt, or leave it on the windowsill in the sun. Next, attune the pendulum to your own energy; since it works through vibration and resonance, it works better if it's cleared of all energy except for yours. Carry it in your pocket for a day to attune the pendulum to your own energy.

Find Your Yes/No/I-Don't-Know. The point of using a pendulum is to quickly receive a yes, no, or I-don't-know-answer to your questions. To determine your pendulum's yes/no/I-don't-know answer, follow these steps:

1. Put your elbow on a table and hold the chain or string of the pendulum between your thumb and first finger. Don't drape it over your finger, just hold it between your thumb and forefinger. Some people find better accuracy when they use their nondominant hand for this. I like keeping the chain short, maybe five or six inches long. You can tuck the rest of the chain into your palm if it's longer than that.

2. Ask your pendulum to show you a yes. It might swing back and forth, around in a circle, or stay perfectly still. This is your yes answer. You can test this by asking a question that you know the answer to. In my case, I might ask, "Is my name Lisa?"

3. Ask your pendulum to show you a no. For me, yes is around in a circle and no is back and forth, but find out what it is for you. Check this against a question that you know has a no answer.

4. Now ask it to show you the "I-don't-know" movement.

5. For any of these questions, you might get no movement or chaotic movement, in a circle, clockwise or counterclockwise, or back and forth. There is no right way for the pendulum to swing, only what is right for you. Ideally, we want a consistent and distinctive movement for yes, no, and I don't know.

Many people go through this every time they use their pendulum, which is totally fine. Mine, however, has been consistent for many years.

Observing how the pendulum swings gives you an immediate yes/no/I-don't-know answer, which is very useful when we want to confirm or deny a psychic hit. Let's say, for example, that you wake up in the middle of the night and you sense the presence of a spirit around you. Your first impression is that it is your Uncle Fred, who recently passed away, but you soon begin to doubt your hit. You can use your pendulum to get instant confirmation on whether it really is Uncle Fred or not. Your pendulum might give you a strong yes that it is Uncle Fred, so you know your first hit was correct. Or maybe it isn't Uncle Fred. You can then use a series of questions to find out who or what was there. Over time, using the pendulum as confirmation really helps us to build our confidence that we are getting accurate psychic impressions.

How and Why Does a Pendulum Work?

Pendulums work in a few different ways. The pendulum "reads" the energy that is around it, first by picking up on your energy so that your own inner guidance will come through it. In this case, your own energy field moves the pendulum. It's also easy for our guides to speak to us directly through it. Pendulums are excellent for reading the energy of people, places, and things, which is a psychic skill called *dowsing*. Reading energy in this way is perhaps the best, most accurate, and most useful application of a pendulum.

I remember being a teenager and using a pendulum as a divination tool. It was my favorite one (next to my Magic 8 Ball). I would ask it quite complex questions and always be sadly disappointed when it was inaccurate. "Does the person that I am crushing on like me, or do they like someone else?" "Are they my one true soul mate?" and "Am I going to get invited to the party?" If I didn't like the answer, I would ask over and over again until the pendulum stopped working all together. I could practically feel my spirit guides rolling their eyes and recommending that I just live in the moment.

There is a reason why this strategy isn't successful. Pendulums have limitations as a divination tool, since it's almost impossible to break down our complex human experiences into binary yes/no equations. This is why we add the "I don't know" option, since there are many things that are unknowable. Our realities are too complex to be broken down into a simple yes/no, so we must add in the possibility that the question you ask is unknowable in the moment. But for our purposes, we will ask very clear questions of it—questions that are specifically about getting confirmation of your psychic impressions. And the trick is to ask *very* specific yes/no questions. "Is this presence that I feel Uncle Fred?" is a great yes/no question. Be mindful that you don't ask multiple questions rolled into one, like "Is this Uncle Fred, or someone else?" Two-part questions will yield inaccurate results.

Be careful not to become dependent on the pendulum, or any divination tool, to make decisions about your own life. I have seen people discover this tool and then start to abdicate their decisions about their own lives to the pendulum. You know that you have gone over the edge if you ask the pendulum if you should wear the blue shirt or the red one today, or if you should have pizza or Chinese food for dinner. We need to continue to be the captains of our lives, make our decisions, and not give our power away to a divination tool.

> ## PSYCHIC TIP: *Pendulum Practice—*
> ## *Try Closing Your Eyes*
>
> If you are worried that your own mind, opinions, hopes, and fears are impacting and manipulating the pendulum, try doing it with your eyes closed. Always begin with one of the grounding and centering practices that I will share in the next chapter. Take a few clearing breaths. Ask your question, being as specific as you can, and then close your eyes. Once you feel the pendulum move, you can open your eyes to see what it is doing. This helps take our own mind out of the equation and gives a cleaner answer.

We've learned some really valuable skills on how to trust your psychic impressions. Now let's talk about how and when to share the psychic information that you receive.

The Ethics of Sharing Psychic Information

As we awaken our psychic abilities, it is absolutely critical to learn how to ethically share this information and, more importantly, when *not* to share. It's our responsibility to behave and speak ethically with our psychic information. And sadly, many psychics are not trained in this crucial aspect of it. I have seen people's friendships, partnerships, and lives damaged and even destroyed by the misuse of psychic information.

It could happen to any of us. One day you are hanging out with your friend, enjoying your time together, when out of the blue, a big download of psychic information about your friend lands on you. Let's say your friend is complaining about their marriage, and all of the sudden something like this pops into your awareness: *You are getting divorced in a few months; the writing is on the wall. And oh my gosh, your spouse may not be actually staying late at work all those nights!* And you get a flash of the lies coming up to the surface and a brief glimpse of you holding your friend's hand through divorce court.

Now, it might not take a psychic to see that coming, but the point is, what do we do with this information? The short answer is say absolutely nothing, unless you are directly asked—and maybe not even then. What happens if you blurt it all out without being asked? What happens if you are wrong? You will have done damage to a friendship that may not be able to be repaired.

Honestly, the very best psychics in the world are only accurate about 80 percent of the time, so we need to be very mindful of what we say. There is no such thing as 100 percent accuracy in a psychic reading, and many factors play into the information that we get. Sometimes as psychics, we are reading someone's feelings, hopes, and fears rather than a hard truth. And there are many factors that come together to create our reality: we all have our free-will choices, our own destiny and karma, and so does everyone else.

As a psychic, I see the moments of choice in front of people, those times when they are at a crossroads in their lives and they have to choose what they are going to do. But I can never really see beyond those choice points, since they are legitimate choices that everyone has to make, and for the most part, those choices are made in the moment.

You might be picking up on the feelings or fears of your friend. You might be able to feel the power of the upcoming crossroad that the couple is facing, but you have no real way of knowing what is going to happen next, since they must choose, and these choices tend to be made in the moment as people live them. Maybe there is really nothing going on. Maybe they'll get counseling and work it all out. Maybe it's projection, and you are projecting your own marriage issues onto your friend.

And, of course, we must acknowledge our own stake in it all. It's very difficult to become totally neutral about these things and to completely drop our own agenda. It's our best friend we are talking about here! We have our own opinions, triggers, feelings, morals, and agenda, we just do. And these mix in with our psychic impressions and color it all. This is why it's very hard to read for ourselves and those that are closest to us.

We also must be mindful of the power in our words, so we need to be careful and honor that what we say, especially if we are sharing a psychic hit, has the power to impact people for their own good or to damage them. It may, in fact, have the power to change the outcome of the situation just because you shared that psychic hit. Maybe they would have worked out their issues, but because you said what you said, their relationship takes a more difficult and darker path, especially if you were wrong. People who believe in psychic information may give extra weight to what you are saying and may begin to create that reality in their lives if they believe it enough.

In this case, to keep our own agenda out of it, we might say something like this: "I sense there is a shift coming in your relationship," which opens it up to any of those possibilities and is a whole world different than something like "Your husband is cheating and you will be getting divorced any minute now."

To sum it all up and to make sure that you are using your psychic skills ethically, without causing harm, here are the psychic ethical rules that I live by:

- I don't share information unless I am asked—no blurting out psychic information without someone's express permission. This is a huge invasion of their privacy, and it is unethical.

- If I am asked and I am not in the right mode to work, I set a boundary and say no. If I am not in the right mind-set to work, I might not get an accurate hit. Saying no is also for my own well-being, since it's not cool to be on call and working all the time.

- The power of our words is mighty and has the possibility to heal or to harm, and it is our responsibility to be mindful of our words.

Ethics are crucial for our life and work as psychics. Because of that, let's break these ethical guidelines down a bit more.

No Psychic Hit-and-Runs

A *psychic hit-and-run* happens when you blurt out psychic information to an unsuspecting person without first getting their permission to do this. People have a right to privacy, and the more we open up our psychic gifts, the greater the responsibility we have to honor the free will of other people. Sadly, there are many people who have strong psychic skills and no idea that they are behaving in an unethical manner that harms others.

Amanda, a young mother in a small rural town, is one of my psychic students who had a painful and humiliating encounter with a psychic hit-and-run. One day she went to the hair salon. The stylist who was doing her hair had tons of natural psychic ability and no training at all on boundaries and ethics.

✴ AMANDA'S STORY *She blurted out every personal detail she was picking up about me and my family in a very loud voice, in a very crowded salon in a very small town. The worst of it was that she was right about a lot of it, but I didn't need everyone to hear all the details, like the fact that my husband and I are in couples therapy and that one of our children is having some emotional and behavioral issues at school. Now the whole town knows. I was so humiliated that I will never go back there, and our friendship is over for good. She was surprised that I was angry with her. She really wanted me to tell her what a great psychic she was, but she hadn't thought at all about what the impact of what she said had on me and my family.*

Do not share psychic information without asking first. And maybe not even then.

I live and breathe by a "don't share unless they ask" policy that I stick to like glue. Honestly, I would have no friends at all if I blurted out every psychic hit I got about my kids, my friends, and my family. Because I work as a professional psychic, I tell all my friends upfront what my policy is and explain to them that I am not going to share my psychic hits with them, unless they specifically ask for them. And guess what? They hardly ever do.

Of course, the exception to this is when I am working and doing client sessions. Then I will share what I am receiving, but even then, I continue to ask my client's permission if it looks like things are going to get deep and could trigger something for them. "Your mother is here, do you want to talk to her?" I don't assume that is a yes without asking. "I am seeing a past life, and it's pretty rough. Do you want to hear about it?" This gives my clients a chance to choose—and choose again—if they are willing and able to receive what I am seeing.

The idea that the hit-and-run psychic reading is acceptable comes from watching psychics on TV. In these shows, the psychic walks into a shop and appears to give a message to a random person. That person is thrilled to receive a message from their loved one, and everyone cries a few happy tears. Let's remember that this entire situation is set up and staged from the get-go. Even if the reading is real, that person is not random, but has chosen to have that experience, has practiced and rehearsed it, and has signed pages of waivers and permissions beforehand. The spontaneity of it is an illusion.

I have done way too much cleanup work for people who got run over, psychically speaking, by bad psychics or even good psychics with no ethical training. For example, one of my clients went to a psychic and was told that she had cancer and the doctors would never find it. This person was so scared and freaked out that, even after the doctors gave her a clean bill of health, she was in a lot of emotional turmoil about the possibility that it could still be there.

Maintain Your Own Boundaries

The other side of the coin on these ethical rules concerns how we treat ourselves. It's important to maintain our own boundaries so that people don't expect us to perform psychic sessions anytime they happen to need or want one. You want to enjoy your friendships and not be a free twenty-four-hour psychic hotline for your pals. It's wise to be crystal clear about this right from the get-go: friends are friends and clients are clients, and that is my boundary. I do, of course, make exceptions for my friends if they ask and I am feeling it. I imagine the situation is similar for people who are lawyers, doctors, or therapists. We don't ask them for free information and services at all hours, right? Like us, they must learn early on how to keep the professional boundary nice and clean.

PSYCHIC TIP: *Asking for Permission to Share*

Sometimes we do run into a situation where we really feel compelled to share our psychic messages with people. If that does happen, then it's crucial to ask for permission to share before you blurt something out. It can be as easy as saying, "Hey, I am not sure how you feel about this type of thing, but I got a psychic message for you and I was wondering if you are open to hearing it." And then respect the person's no if you get one.

Now that we have covered the ethics of how to manage the psychic information that we are receiving, let's move on to another important topic: turning our psychic abilities on and off at will. How do we do that?

Turning Your Psychic Abilities On and Off

One of the key foundational skills that we all need is understanding how to turn our abilities on and off. Many psychic students are frustrated by either feeling flooded or overwhelmed by psychic messages that they don't need or want in that moment. Let's say you are in the market—I am just here to buy veggies!—but you become flooded with psychic and empathic information from all the people around you. This can easily drain your energy and overwhelm you with what I call "psychic static."

Or perhaps you are on the other side of the fence and you feel frustrated because you might be coming up dry in a situation when you really do need to receive some psychic information. It's easy to feel annoyed when you really need and want some psychic information but just can't seem to connect on demand.

Once I was at a busy restaurant with a friend of mine who said something along the lines of "It must be so cool to be able to know stuff about all these people!" But the truth of it is that unless you can turn off your psychic perceptions at will, it's like the world's biggest, most painful case of constant TMI—too much information.

And for many newly awakened psychic students, their abilities seem to blink on and off at random. They are full on just when you don't want it and nowhere to be found when you do. For me, it's a matter of having a good energetic boundary and the sheer willpower to turn my attention to other things. Imagine that you are sitting at a bar with someone and there is a TV playing just behind their head. You can use your willpower to direct your attention to the person you are talking to and ignore what is on the TV. Turning off psychic impressions can be a lot like that.

Here are some other great ways to practice turning your psychic abilities on and off. Try them on for size, see which ones work for you, and then practice, practice, practice until they become second nature.

Turning Them On

If you want to open up your psychic abilities even more, you have a number of options. Here are some great ways to turn up your ability to tune in:

- Take a deep breath into your heart or belly and bring your attention inward. Imagine that there is a blank receptive place inside, like an empty blackboard, and see what arises in that space. Try asking a question before you do this to see if you get an answer.

- Try automatic writing, which is when we write a question down and then go into a quiet, receptive, meditative space. Write down the answers you get without thinking about them too much.

- Light a small white candle like a tea light to signify that you are open to receiving messages and then blow it out when you are done. This candle lighting can be added to any of the other suggestions given here. It gives a distinct boundary about when you are open to receiving and when you are not. Any other small ritual can be used instead of a candle.

- Put your hands together at your heart and say, "My psychic senses are now fully open, and I am open to receiving guidance." When you are done and want to shut things down say, "My psychic senses are now closed. Thank you for the guidance that I received."

- Feel gratitude when you do get a psychic hit, and you will receive more and more.

Make sure to record anything that you received in your psychic journal and to celebrate your successes. Much of opening up is about relaxing, letting yourself feel and perceive things, and then paying attention to what you perceive. Remember that being overly analytical and critical of yourself will shut you down quickly, so try to have fun, relax, and open up your feelings.

Turning Them Off

Some of you, however, will be looking for tools to help you turn off your psychic awareness and set some boundaries around it. We all need a way to turn our psychic senses off when we want some peace and quiet. Mini-rituals and visualizations work well to create boundaries around when it's okay to be psychically open and when it isn't. Here are some good ways to do that:

- Imagine there is a radio or TV inside you that you can turn on and off when you need to. It has a volume dial and an on/off switch. When you want to tone things down, turn the volume dial down. If you want to shut it all the way down, go to the on/off switch and turn it off. I learned this one as a young child and it really works for me, especially with turning off both the visual and auditory psychic senses.

- You can imagine turning a light switch on and off. Or imagine turning the "open" and "closed" signs like you would in a shop so that you are open for business or closed for business.

- If you feel energetically too open, image that you are zipping your energy field closed. Start with your hands down in front of your hips and move your hands up your body, as if you were actually zipping something up. This is a powerful one for empaths when we are out in public.

- Always open with a positive appreciation for your gifts and close with gratitude for whatever guidance you have received.

What's Next?

I hope this has given you a good start in acquiring the foundational skills you need to feel confident in opening up your psychic abilities. Our next step is to learn how to be protected and safe as we continue to open up. Let's delve into the energy management practices that will help keep us centered, grounded, and protected while we are opening up.

Chapter 2

Defend Your Psychic Self

As we open up our psychic abilities, it's also super important to learn to manage our energy and sort out the good psychic energy from the bad. In fact, the more we open, the more important it is to learn how to stay energetically grounded, clear, and protected. These skills are something that all sensitives need to know, and for me, it has been the difference between feeling like a raw nerve that can't leave my house without being overwhelmed emotionally, psychically, and energetically and being confident and strong in the world no matter what I am doing.

When I was studying at university, I took karate classes and earned my black belt a few times over. I loved martial arts, because I never wanted to be afraid of being in the world. Having a good knowledge base and some street smarts can help us as psychic students in being able to open up our psychic skills safely without leaving us vulnerable. We all need a little spiritual kung fu to stay safe out there.

There are two parts of psychic self-defense, and we will cover both in this chapter. The first part is learning how to manage your own energy. This is about making sure that you have good boundaries, that you know how to clear any emotional or psychic energy you might have picked up from other people as well as how to stay grounded and centered so you can be present in the moment. I put all of this together in what I call "energy management practices," and they are a must-have skill set for emerging psychics and especially for empaths.

The second part of psychic self-defense is learning how to protect ourselves from three different things: the intrusive energy of other people, the psychic impact of the environments that we occupy, and potential contact with spiritual beings that may not have our best interests at heart.

I know that when you master these energy management and psychic self-defense skills, you will be able to be open when you want to be and also protected if you have to be out and about in the world.

Energy Management Practices

Let me start by defining what I mean by *energy*; it is literally that, our life force energy, our chi. Since I have been working as an energy medicine practitioner for the over twenty years now, I speak about this topic in terms of our *energy field*. This is the part of us that is more than just our body, mind, and emotions. As psychics, we will work on centering, grounding, and clearing out the energetic and psychic static we pick up from others. We also need skills in replacing our lost life force energy so we don't feel drained, and we need to strengthen our entire energy field so we are more protected and have better boundaries.

Our energy field is made up of our life force energy and has a lot of different parts to it. We have energy centers called *chakras* and also lines of energy called *meridians* that Chinese medicine practitioners use. We will focus more on the layers of our energy field that we call the *aura* and also the part of our energy field that connects us to the earth, which is called the *grounding cord*. For our purposes, we will focus on the two parts that we need most for psychic protection: the grounding cord and the boundary layer of the aura.

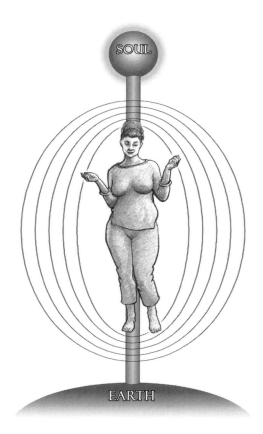

Centering

Let's start with one of the most basic and powerful of these energy management practices—how to get centered. As we go about our day, we tend to scatter our energy and attention outside ourselves and that can make us feel unsettled and ungrounded. Your *center* is the part of your body where you feel like your consciousness resides. This might be the actual center of your body, like your belly, but it's really more about where you feel the locus of your being resides. For some people, it's in their heads, but most people feel their center to be either the heart, the belly, or sometimes below their navel; it is the place inside your body where you feel your selfhood resides.

Centering is practice that allows us to bring those scattered parts of ourselves back home and to reconnect with ourselves. When we lose connection with ourselves, we can feel lost, depressed, and anxious. We get uncentered when our minds and emotions become stuck in something outside ourselves. For example, once you are home, you might still be thinking about work and feeling anxious about it. Centering is a powerful and quick way to manage your energy. Here's how to do it.

Exercise: Finding Your Center

Centering is something that can be done in a few breaths, whenever we notice that we have become disconnected from ourselves. We can center ourselves anytime. (You can download an audio recording of this meditation at http://www.newharbinger .com/50744.)

1. Start with pushing your feet into the floor and taking a deep breath. Closing your eyes can help too.

2. Tap into yourself, and try to find the most essential part of who you are. It can help to remember a time when you felt joyful, at peace, or in the flow of doing something that you really love.

3. Notice if you can connect that feeling of joy and passion to a part of your body. It might be your heart or somewhere in your belly.

4. Without thinking about it too much, put your hands on that place. It can help to say "I am here" as you do this.

5. Now breathe deeply into your center. As you inhale, imagine that you are pulling yourself back into that place, you are pulling all the scattered parts of yourself back into your center.

6. On the exhale, breathe down your legs and out the bottoms of your feet, releasing any stray thoughts and feelings that you are ready to let go of.

7. Repeat this until you feel like your attention and energy are back inside you, and you feel peaceful.

Practice this anytime you feel scattered or disconnected from yourself. Centering is like a muscle that will strengthen over time. Eventually, you can center yourself quickly, anytime and anywhere, by putting your hand on your center, breathing into that part of you, and saying, "I am here."

Now that we have learned to center ourselves, the next step in energy management is learning to *ground*. If centering is getting reconnected to yourself, then grounding is all about reconnecting to the earth. We must take these two essential steps—centering and grounding—so that we can open up our psychic abilities safely and responsibly.

Grounding

Grounding involves being fully in our bodies with our mind in the present moment and connecting to the energy of the earth. The opposite of being grounded is being ungrounded, which we experience as being spacey and unable to focus on the present moment. For example, many sensitive people learn the habit of energetically leaving their bodies, something psychologists call "dissociating."

Empaths often become ungrounded when they hit empathic overload and their senses are swamped with sensory stimulation. As sensitives, our nervous systems get blown out easily by lights, sounds, and the chaos of other people's energy. Places like big box stores or the shops during the holidays blow the circuits in our sensitive nervous system and put us into fight-or-flight mode. The "flight" part of fight-or-flight is this dissociated state.

When we go into flight and dissociate, we may feel a temporary and illusory sense of safety, but dissociation is a nonproductive habit. The truth is you are actually safer if you are fully present in your body. Being in your body and having your mind in the present moment means you can find your power and respond appropriately to whatever situation you are in. This is something that I learned very quickly while I was studying martial arts: if you space out during a sparring match, you will quickly and sometimes painfully lose that match.

To help us ground quickly and efficiently, we are going to practice connecting with a part of our energy anatomy called the *grounding cord.* This cord extends down from our tailbones into the earth and is essential in keeping us grounded.

For many of us, when we go into fight-or-flight, we disconnect from the grounding cord and leave our bodies. Much like a dog does when it tucks in its tail, we become disconnected from our grounding cord when we go into fear. Reconnecting with it is a great way to instantly feel more grounded. When we practice this on a regular basis, it can, over time, help us change our habit of being ungrounded.

Exercise: Reconnecting with the Grounding Cord

In order to stay grounded, we need to be connected to the earth. Here is a breathing and visualization meditation that can help us reconnect to the earth. (To visualize your grounding cord, use whatever image works for you, but make the cord very wide, as wide as a dinner plate or trash can. You may want to imagine your grounding cord as the taproot of a big tree or a heavy chain with an anchor on the end of it.) You can download an audio recording of this meditation at http://www.newharbinger.com/50744.

1. Start either by sitting in a chair with your feet on the floor or standing up.

2. If you are sitting, push your feet into the floor.

3. Straighten your spine as much as you can. Slouching tends to create blocks in the central column of energy, known as the *hara line,* which runs up your spine.

4. Take a deep breath in, and imagine a big beam of light coming in the top of your head and traveling all the way down your spine to your tailbone.

5. Drop your energy and attention down to your tailbone, and imagine, pretend, or visualize the grounding cord descending deep into the earth.

6. As you exhale, see how deep you can get your grounding cord to go. Visualize it moving easily through all the layers of the building that you are in and deep down into the earth.

7. You might feel heavier, more solid, and may even feel energy tingling through your legs as you become regrounded.

Do this exercise anywhere and anytime you notice that you are feeling spacy, ungrounded, or unsafe.

We all need lots of tools in our psychic tool kits, so it's wise to have many ways to ground ourselves. In addition to grounding meditations, it's helpful to have some other practical ways to get grounded. I suggest you consider some of the experiences in the list below and then add your own ways to become grounded to this list. In your psychic journal, list the ones that you know work for you and refer back to them when you need more grounding. I incorporate these into my life on a regular basis and am able to manage all the psychic work that I do because of it. Here are some things to try:

• Be outside in nature. Try walking in the woods, on the beach, or in a city park. Gardening is also a great grounding exercise.

• Go barefoot outside. Being barefoot for even a few minutes is very grounding. When it's too cold to go barefoot outside, I have a big river rock under my desk that I put my bare feet on when I am working.

• Do ordinary things like housework, washing the dishes, and taking care of yourself and your environment. If you do these activities mindfully and intentionally, they can be very grounding. Make sure you breathe while you are grounding. Long, slow breathing into your belly can ground you instantly. Practice bringing your breath all the way to your tailbone and then down into the grounding cord. Holding your breath will keep you from being fully grounded.

• Exercising mindfully and joyfully can often put you back in your body. Walking, yoga, lifting weights, or dancing, anything that wakes up your body will do it.

• Carry gemstones like smoky quartz, hematite, obsidian, garnet, or even magnets in your pocket. These are fantastic to help keep you grounded.

- Eat healthy food, drink plenty of water, and get sufficient sleep. These and other aspects of self-care are very grounding. When we take loving care of our bodies, we make it safe and pleasurable to inhabit them.

The more that we open up our psychic abilities, the more important it is to balance that opening with grounding. I love to create that balance in my own life by doing housework, gardening, and taking care of my body and my home environment. After doing hours of psychic readings at my office, it helps to come home and walk my dog in the woods or on the beach, weed the garden, or even wash the kitchen floor.

As we master the art of staying grounded, let's look at the next phase of maintaining our psychic hygiene. This involves learning how to clear ourselves of the energy that we pick up from other people and the places we visit.

Clearing

Clearing is how we remove unwanted energy from our own systems. We constantly pick up energy from other people and places, and as sensitives, we tend to collect it in a way that impacts us negatively.

The more sensitive and empathic you are, the more of an issue this might be for you. Empaths tend to have a spongy, porous energy field. That means that the outer, boundary layer of your energy field is porous like a sponge. Nonempathic people have a more solid boundary layer like an egg shell, so they are a little less prone to picking up energetic gunk.

As we open up our psychic abilities, we become more sensitive to this energetic residue. For the most part, the residue is made up of residual energy and high-impact trauma residue.

Residual Energy. Have you ever walked into a room after people have been arguing there? We can feel anger, hatred, resentment, sadness, frustration, and grief all trapped in that space. This residual energy is made up of emotions, thoughts, psychic and life force energy, and it can linger in our environments. It's most often intense or negative energy that sticks with us. (See the section below on space clearing to learn how to remove this.)

High-Impact Trauma Residue. This is the emotional and energetic residue from places where bad things have happened—crime scenes, battlefields, hospitals, courthouses, jails, and any other place where trauma has occurred.

These places carry an imprint of the emotions and energy of that trauma, and sensitives not only feel it but also absorb it.

As we move about in the world and encounter this residual energy, we need to clear it from our bodies, emotions, and energy fields. Here is an example of how energetic clearing can impact someone sensitive.

Camille works as a guidance counselor in a busy, urban junior high school. She recently shared me with me how she has applied the clearing techniques that she learned from me so she can remain functional as a sensitive in a challenging environment. Camille said that she knows she needs clearing when she starts feeling fatigued, has brain fog, or has emotional swings. Camille also ends her day with another quick clearing regime before she goes to bed.

✴ CAMILLE'S STORY   *A junior high school in a big city is a tough place for a sensitive like me. The students are stressed out to the max, and everyone is going through puberty, so emotions are on overdrive, and they have not figured out yet how to manage them. As the guidance counselor, I get all the troubled students and disciplinary issues to handle, so my day-to-day work is emotionally charged. I find that all the parents and fellow teachers are also totally stressed, depressed, and anxious. It's like swimming in a toxic soup of emotions and energy.*

I just start feeling off. I am either so tired that I could put my head down on my desk and sleep, or I feel angry, sad, or cranky for no reason. If that happens, I know I picked up some emotions and energy from my students or fellow faculty members. It can hit me out of the blue, but I often know where and when I picked up energy that is not mine, and I know it's time to clear myself.

I clear myself many times during the day. I start with a morning meditation and use my morning shower to clear myself too. By the time lunch rolls around, I go outside and walk around a little. I do some of the clearing breaths outside and take lunch outside, weather permitting. This helps me get through the rest of my afternoon. After work, I sit in my car and do the clearing breaths again so I don't bring all that junk home with me.

If it's been a really tough day, I might take a salt bath before bed, or use some sage to smudge myself, but I at least check myself and make sure I am really clear before bed.

These clearing rituals have helped Camille keep functioning in the work that she loves. They enable her to do that work without it taking too much of a toll on her sensitive system.

Exercise: Energy Clearing Ritual

This is my go-to quick clearing ritual. Use this powerful clearing technique anytime you feel impacted by energetic overload. You can download an audio recording of this meditation at http://www.newharbinger.com/50744.

1. Start with the centering and grounding cord meditations to get centered and grounded.

2. As you settle into yourself, notice if there is a place in your system that feels tense or restricted. Many people hold energy that needs to be cleared in either their hearts or their bellies, but it could be anywhere. See if you can notice where it is.

3. As you inhale, use your breath to bring light to wherever you feel the energetic residue in your system.

4. As you exhale, imagine that the energy gunk is flushing down the grounding cord into the earth. We always want to thank the earth and ask that the gunk be transformed. (Think compost.)

5. You can also pull energy up from the earth and blow any energetic gunk out the top of your head, if this feels more natural to you.

Do this every time you feel your system is clogged with energetic residue.

Energetic clearing is really all about changing our habit of absorbing other people's energy and holding on to it. As we practice energy clearing regularly, we're developing, over time, better psychic hygiene. It's like when you need to do a really deep spring cleaning on your house. If it's been a while, the house is probably really dirty and everything needs a thorough cleaning. But if you keep up with the dirt regularly, you have a lot less work to do.

Other Ways to Clear Energy

It's useful to have other ways to clear energy in addition to the Energy Clearing Ritual above. We don't always have time and space to do this meditation and breathing practice, so having many tools in our psychic tool kit can help when something else is called for. Let's look at some other ways to do energetic clearing.

Water. Water is one of the best ways to clear ourselves. When you are in the shower, imagine the water washing away any residual energy that you don't need anymore. I sometimes do this quickly just by washing my hands and saying, "With this water, I release any energy that is not mine." Try a salt bath, using any kind of salt. I like sea salt or Epsom salts. You can also use a salt scrub in the shower. State your intention to clear energy residue as you do this.

Salt. One of the best purifiers around, salt naturally absorbs negative energy. As well as using it in your bath, try keeping a bowl of salt under your bed to keep yourself clear while you are sleeping. Salt lamps are made from big chunks of Himalayan salt that are set on a light base. They are widely available these days and are very effective ways to clear your environments. They also make great night-lights for sensitive children. I often wonder if the purifying quality of salt is where the idea of throwing salt over your shoulder to clear the evil eye came from.

Smudge Yourself. Try using aromatic smoke, like sage, sweetgrass, palo santo, or incense. Use a feather to waft the smoke through your aura or through your environment. Try a spray sage, if you are in a place where you can't burn something.

Sound. Sound frequencies can easily break up stuck energy. Try singing, chanting, or praying out loud. Listening to music that enlivens us can clear our energy. Pair this with singing or dancing to the music for added clearing—and more fun too! Also drums, rattles, bells, and tuning forks are great tools to add to your tool kit. A small 528 Hz tuning fork works wonders. I travel with one to clear hotel rooms and Airbnbs. You can even clear a space by clapping loudly and stating out loud your intention to clear out old, stuck energy. It could be why we were told to whistle when we pass a graveyard.

Sweating. Working up a good sweat is also a great way to clear yourself. Try a steam shower, a sauna, sweat lodge, or even a hot yoga class. Or do any exercise that makes you breathe and sweat.

Essential Oils. There are many essential oils that work wonders for energetic clearing. Some of the best cleansing oils include lemongrass, cypress, lemon, frankincense, eucalyptus, grapefruit, rosemary, and peppermint. Try them in a diffuser to clear your space, or put some in your salt bath to add a wonderful fragrance.

Running Water. For your environments, try some running water. Fountains and fish tanks with a filter cleanse our environments and not only tend to clear residual energy but also to keep away spirits. Try them in kids' rooms if your children are getting unwelcome nighttime visitations from spirits. Standing on a bridge over running water works wonders, and so does standing near the seashore.

The Golden Circle Clearing. This is a quick and powerful variation of the clearing ritual. Center and ground yourself. Now imagine a golden circle, like a hula hoop, hovering over your head. Visualize that the circle is filled with golden light. You can start the circle either at your feet or your head, and imagine—as your body moves through the circle and the light fills you up—that it's clearing out any and all residual energy.

PSYCHIC TIP: *Your Best Energy Clearing Techniques*

Think of a few things that you know work for you when you need to center, ground, and clear yourself. Make a list of these in your psychic journal, and find a way to weave these things into your daily life. This is how we transform the habit of poor psychic hygiene into our daily self-care rituals.

Space Clearing

As we continue to open to our psychic abilities, we can become more and more sensitive to the energies present in the physical spaces that we occupy. Learning how to energetically clear your house, office, hotel room, or wherever you are is a must-have skill for all empaths and psychically sensitive people.

Carlos recently moved into a condo in a lovely development in California. He called me for a consultation shortly after he moved in.

✳ CARLOS'S STORY   *I couldn't figure out why this one unit was so cheap and why it had been empty for so long. I was thrilled to get it and at such a good price too. Shortly after I moved in, my neighbors told me that the family who lived there had a series of tragedies that included family members experiencing financial loss due to a catastrophic illness, chronic depression, and even a suicide. The condo definitely has a sad and lonely feeling, and I have been uncomfortable living there.*

As a sensitive, Carlos was tuned in to the residual energy of his new condo and all the events that had happened before he arrived there. It needed to be cleared of all the residual energy and probably of the lingering spirit of the person who committed suicide. Carlos used the space-clearing technique below and moved the old stuck energy out.

Exercise: No-Fail Space-Clearing Protocol

This is a powerful and easy way to remove lingering energy and spirits. You can use it anywhere, and I recommended adding these tools to your travel kit so you can clear hotel rooms and Airbnbs too.

1. Begin by centering and grounding yourself.

2. Open all the windows and doors to let in light and air, and clear any clutter. Clutter tends to build up where there is stuck energy, so clearing clutter before you begin is helpful. Giving your space a good cleaning is also super helpful.

3. If you can burn something, use sage and mix it in a small cast-iron skillet with the white papery coverings of garlic and also some salt. A sage stick or bundle will also work very well. Look for white sagebrush and not the culinary sage that we use for cooking.

4.   If you can't burn something, then mix a spray bottle full of water with salt and some sage essential oil. You can also use peppermint, grapefruit, or lemon essential oil. I throw in some holy or blessed water too. If you would rather not use sage at all, you can do this same technique with a bell or tuning fork instead of the sage.

5.   Begin inside at the front door and either sage, spray, or ring your bell as you move clockwise through your space. Places where clutter collects are often in need of extra clearing. Pay close attention to behind doors and under chairs and tables. Do the closets and definitely the basement and the attic. There is a reason why ghosts always hang out in closets, the basement, and the attic!

6.   As you move through the space, you can pray if you like, or say out loud that you claim this as your space (even if it's for only one night): "*I cleanse this space of all negativity and invite in the energy of love, health, prosperity, and joy.*" You can also invoke your guides, angels, and/or divine beings to assist you: "*In the name of Jesus/Buddha/Allah/Archangel Michael, I call in love and cast out negativity. I invite all spirits to return to the divine now.*"

7.   Once you have gone through the whole space with your sage, spray, or bell, find the energetic center of the space. If it's going to be a long-term home for you, drop the grounding cord down and claim the space as your own.

You can do an abbreviated version of this in places where you will be temporarily, like a hotel room. I have done this with whatever I had on hand, and if you have nothing, then try walking around the space, praying, and clapping your hands with the intention of bringing good energy in and moving bad energy out.

If you feel like your space still needs help after this, it is probably time to call in a professional. You can have your house blessed by a clergyperson like a priest, minister, rabbi, or imam. Most faith traditions have house blessing ceremonies that work wonders. There are also feng shui experts and professional psychics that specialize in moving along stuck spirits.

That is what Carlos needed to do to completely clear his space. He told me, "I tried the sage, and it definitely cleared out the lingering sadness that was in the condo, but I needed more help to remove the spirits there." Carlos opted to have a house blessing, and a pastor came in to bless the house and remove any wayward spirits. His condo has been a peaceful and joyful refuge for him ever since.

Let's move to the last stage of our psychic hygiene. We will now learn how to protect and shield ourselves.

Psychic Protection

Now that we have learned to center, ground, and clear ourselves, the last stage of psychic hygiene is self-protection. We can sum this up by saying that psychic protection is all about learning to set boundaries. It's a difficult skill for many sensitives to master, but the good news is that once we learn how to set a boundary, it works in all the situations that we might find ourselves. Once we learn the art of setting boundaries, we can move freely about the world feeling safe, confident, and protected. For a deep dive into this topic, I recommend my book *Energy Healing for Empaths: How to Protect Yourself from Energy Vampires, Honor Your Boundaries, and Build Healthier Relationships*.[1] The whole book is dedicated to learning many different ways to set boundaries.

The Boundary Layer

For students of psychic development, the most important boundary is the one located at the very outer edge of our energy field. This is the boundary between ourselves and the world. It's the energetic equivalent of your skin, which protects you from the outer world. Your skin keeps out toxins, germs, and other harmful things, but it also allows in things that we need. This boundary layer of your aura does the same thing on an energetic level.

The more empathic and sensitive you are, the more likely this boundary is porous and spongy, creating a wishy-washy delineation between you, other people, and the world. Thankfully, this part of our energy anatomy is very responsive to our intentions and visualization, so one of the easiest and most efficient ways to strengthen it is to do a breathing and visualizing meditation. This is my go-to psychic protection technique.

Exercise: Creating a Protection Bubble

This can be done in a few breaths, anywhere and anytime you feel like you need some psychic protection. I use it when I need to go to crowded places, or anywhere there are a lot of people and chaotic energy. I have also done it in dicey social situations and at times when there is chaotic angry and hostile energy around. (You can download an audio recording of this meditation at http://www.newharbinger.com/50744.)

1. Start with one or two centering breaths.

2. Connect to the grounding cord and see if you can feel the energy flowing all the way down your spine, and from your tailbone to your feet.

3. As you inhale, pull energy strongly into your center. It's great if you can pull up from the earth and down from divine source at the same time.

4. Collect this energy at your center, and as you exhale, breathe this light out through your body and through all the layers of your energy field right out to the boundary layer and beyond.

5. Imagine that the boundary layer is something strong. Use whatever image comes to mind: a rubber ball, a crystal ball, a bowling ball, or even a castle wall.

6. See it, feel it, sense it, or just know that you are on the inside of the bubble. The world is on the other side and nothing can cross this boundary without your permission.

7. Set your intention that only supportive energy comes through this boundary layer and nonsupportive energy stays on the other side. Nothing can cross this boundary without your permission.

Doing this regularly and over time will permanently strengthen your boundary layer. It's much like going to the gym on a regular basis will give you a stronger and more resilient physique.

Once we have a good strong energetic boundary, that is often enough to help us feel like we can start setting boundaries in other ways. Having good boundaries means knowing when and how to say no, and it works just the same for people and spirits.

As sensitives, we often feel like we don't have a right to say no to others and that we must be at everyone's beck and call. You have the right to say no to any request or demand that anyone makes of you. If you get a demand from someone and you are not sure how you feel about it, take a few centering breaths and see if you can feel if this is right for you or not.

When someone asks me for something, I almost never give my answer in the moment. I have learned to tell people that I need to check my calendar and that I will get back to them the next day. I get centered and grounded and then check within myself and see if it's a yes or a no.

Learning a few ways to say a very polite no will assist you in having clear boundaries too. If you are firm, polite, and consistent, people (and spirits too) will learn to respect your boundaries over time. I favor a "no, thank you" without overly explaining and stick to that.

Once your boundaries are stronger and clearer, you can further strengthen your energy field (and therefore also your boundary) by living a clean, healthy lifestyle. Having an unhealthy lifestyle weakens the boundary layer of our energy field and makes us more vulnerable to intrusive energies.

Here are two examples of what I am talking about—these are not real people, by the way, but rather an amalgam of many people that I have encountered over the years. I use these fictional examples just to illustrate my point and show you how much your lifestyle choices can impact your psychic self-defense.

Tanner exemplifies how living a healthy life helps his psychic self-defense. He is a yoga instructor who gets on the yoga mat every day. He is dedicated to his practice and also meditates both on and off the mat. Tanner enjoys a clean diet of whole foods and stays away from chemicals and heavily processed foods, which have a tendency to impact and weaken our whole system, but especially to weaken the boundary layer of our energy field. He walks his dog in the woods every day too and feels rejuvenated by breathing fresh air and communing with nature. He uses this time to consciously clear his energy field and release all the residual energy he has picked up.

Tanner has had his fair share of issues and traumas in his life, but has spent a lot of time and energy dealing with his past. He's learned how to handle his emotions on a daily basis as they come up. He journals, gets therapy when he needs it, and focuses on finding productive ways to express his feelings. His yoga and meditation practice has helped to open up his psychic abilities very quickly, but he feels happy and excited about it: "I set a strong intention of only communicating with my angels and the highest level guides that are available to me. I have learned how to say no to lower vibrational energies, whether it's my food, other people's stuff, or the lower vibration spirits. And I know that my psychic gifts are meant to help other people." Tanner told me that he feels calm and happy about his psychic opening and has positive experiences that uplift and guide him through his own life and assist him in being of service to others.

On the other hand, we have Mika, who has been struggling with depression and anxiety for most of his life. He is an empath but hasn't yet figured out how to manage his energy, so he feels at the mercy of his emotional states. Like Tanner, he also had childhood trauma but he hasn't yet addressed it, and his unhealed trauma and unprocessed emotions add to his depression and anxiety.

Mika learned some bad habits that still get the better of him. He eats poorly, focusing on chemical-laden fast foods and convenience foods, and he admits to being a couch potato. He doesn't exercise or spend much time out in nature, but he does watch a lot of TV. He loves paranormal TV shows and is fascinated by the dark side of these, choosing shows about demons, possessions, and extreme and violent hauntings.

Mika admits to having used a Ouija board many times as well as doing séances to speak to the dead. His apartment is haunted to the rafters, since he occasionally holds séances there and has accidently opened a portal to the dodgy side of Over There. Wayward and earthbound spirits wander through on a regular basis, attracted to his wishy-washy boundaries and his internal and unprocessed inner turmoil.

He has recently begun to work with a ghost-hunting team doing paranormal investigation. Unfortunately, they are mostly amateurs who don't practice good psychic self-defense techniques before they investigate. Mika thinks he brought home an entity with him from their last visit to the abandoned mental hospital where they also brought the Ouija board during a full moon. On Halloween.

Sadly, I have worked with many people that are pretty close to poor Mika's situation, but my point here is that we can open up safely if we use common sense, have good boundaries, and live a clean, healthy life. Or we can be like Mika and attract the dark stuff and suffer the consequences. Don't be like Mika.

Psychic Protection Basics

Let's look now at the psychic protection basics that will help you stay clear of the dark side. Good psychic self-defense isn't complicated, if we use common sense. It's a lot like being street smart. We want to do what we know is helpful and good, and stay away from risky behaviors.

Please do these things:

- Live a healthy life by taking care of yourself. Self-care like eating and sleeping well and getting plenty of exercise helps keeps our vibration high.

- Learn to handle your emotions as they arise on a daily basis and clean up any past trauma, if you need to.

- Practice the basic ground, clear, and protect rituals on a daily basis.

- Work on your boundaries and learn when and where to say no.

- Commit to a spiritual practice like yoga or meditation. Your spiritual practice will protect you and make you stronger.

Please don't do these things:

- Don't engage in high-risk psychic activities, like Ouija or other spirit boards, séances, table tipping, or other things that call in the spirits of the dead, unless you are properly trained in how to do this.

- Ghost hunting is a high-risk psychic activity. It can be done safely, but you really need to know what you are doing. Get proper training and don't go alone.

- Don't look too far into the darkness or go looking for trouble. Don't conjure demons, and don't engage in black magic or blood rituals.

- Excessive and addictive drug or alcohol use shreds your energy field. It also attracts entities and can make you attractive to darker energies. Definitely don't mix excessive drinking and drug use with psychic or paranormal activities.

If you follow these commonsense rules, you should be fine. We really need to look for trouble to find it. Set your intention to stay in the light and choose to stay out of the darker side of things.

What's Next?

I hope that you now have a good sense of the foundational skills that all of us psychics need to know in order to really manage our psychic opening with grace and confidence rather than fear. As you practice these skills, I know you are going to gain more control over your gifts so that you will have them at your fingertips when you need them. Let's move on now to understanding what our psychic senses are and how to maximize them.

Chapter 3

Open Your Psychic Senses

Our psychic senses are open channels through which we receive our intuitive and psychic information. When our psychic senses are open, we receive our psychic impressions with ease, and we know how to integrate and make meaning of them. They enhance and add to our physical senses, bringing another layer of meaning to our lives. When we have mastered opening our psychic senses, we experience psychic impressions seamlessly, without fear. It can even help us to live more joyfully in the world as we live by our own psychic guidance.

In order to understand what the senses are, let's bring up a term that is an oldie but goodie. I love the term ESP (extrasensory perception). The idea behind ESP is that people who are psychic have more access than other people to their sensory intake.

Our brains constantly take in sensory data. At any given time, we are experiencing our immediate environment through our five senses. We learn from a young age to filter out the sensory data that is not relevant to what we are doing at the moment.

As you read this book, your mind is concentrating on the text and you are subconsciously filtering out the sensory experiences that are not relevant to this task. You are not focused on the way that your clothes feel on your skin, the taste in your mouth, or the physical sensations of your digestive system. Perhaps you are also filtering out any background noise and putting your emotional reactions on the back burner while you concentrate.

In order to focus and concentrate, we put our attention on something like a spotlight. The theory of ESP is that psychics actually widen the lenses of their senses and so process more sensory data than other people do. I think that is true, but I also think that our sensors are more sensitive than the sensors of others and that we are picking up forms of energy that are not available to other people. Perhaps as psychics, we pick up more subtle energies and frequencies that other people have yet to learn to pay attention to. And yet, there is a distinction between our physical senses and our psychic senses.

The Psychic Senses

When we have a psychic experience, chances are good that it's with our psychic senses rather than our physical senses. Our *psychic senses* are an extension of our physical senses into the nonordinary world, so we perceive things like energy, different states of time (like the past and the future), and the presence spiritual beings.

These are the *clairs,* as some people call them. For example, if you are *clairvoyant,* you have the visual psychic sense. There might be times when you actually see things with your real eyes, but most of your clairvoyant perceptions will be like seeing things with your inner eye, much like having a daydream or visualizing something.

When I was a kid, I would sometimes see things with my physical eyes. This means there were occasions that I was not able to distinguish between the spirit of a person and an actual living person. The spirits appeared solid to me, like I could reach out and touch them.

Quite frankly, I hated this experience, and when I was young, I made a conscious decision to turn this part of my gift off. It's one of the most challenging psychic gifts to have, and there are times that it still happens to me. I have had conversations with people that only I could see. If I was with friends when this happened, my friends would look a little queasy and back away from me slowly.

Not too long ago, I came into my office a little early on a Monday morning only to find an elderly man sitting in my client chair with a shy smile. I was startled and was trying to figure out how he got into my office. Did I forget to lock the front door?

"Excuse me, sir, can I help you?" I asked. He gave me a little nod and wink, and then slowly faded out, Cheshire cat–style. I heard his voice in my head as he apologized for startling me. He was waiting for my 9 a.m. client to arrive since he had some messages and some unfinished business to clear up. He was so real looking to me that I did not that know he was a spirit until he faded away. This is an example of having a psychic experience with your physical eyes rather than your psychic eyes.

I still don't enjoy the experience of seeing spirits with my physical eye, and prefer to see things with my *psychic eye.* When I was little, I called this my imagination eye. When we use our psychic senses, it's more like the experience is happening inside our own heads, and the visions happen on the inner screen inside our minds. It might seem like you are imagining or having a daydream because the visions are little movies playing on the screen of your psychic eye rather than your physical eye.

In all the years that I have been doing psychic readings for people, I have come to realize that I see the physical world with my right eye and the psychic world with my left eye. This is interesting to me since the left eye is connected to the right brain and that would be the more psychic part of my brain. I can use one eye to view what is happening psychically, and through the other eye, I am engaged with my client. It's taken me many years to master this sort of binocular seeing, but it works for me.

There are many psychic senses besides just the visual sense. Let's look at them briefly now.

The Body Sense. Psychic impressions are experienced as physical sensations like shivers, gooseflesh, tingles, or a happy (or queasy) stomach. We feel it all in our bodies.

Clairsentience—The Feeling Sense. We feel our psychic impressions as a combination of emotions and sensations: "*I have a good feeling about this!*" We *feel* things.

Claircognizance—The Knowing Sense. This is our inner knowing. It is often felt in our gut and can bypass our mind's knowing: "*I don't know how I know, I just do.*"

Clairalience and Clairgustance—The Smell and Taste Senses. We smell and taste things that are not physically present. Since this psychic sense is the most linked to our memory, it often comes up when our departed loved ones are around. We might, for example, smell the pipe smoke that was our grandfather's signature scent. Or we might taste the special dish that a beloved relative created for special occasions. My friend Jody always knows her mother is around her when she can taste the coconut cream cake her mom always made for her birthdays.

Clairaudience—The Auditory Sense. We can hear psychic phenomenon as if it were a voice inside our own heads. Sometimes we hear things out loud too.

Clairvoyance—The Visual Sense. You will experience your psychic hits in a visual way. It might be colors and energy around people or things, or as movies that are playing on the screen of your mind.

Some people have a few of these that are very strong, but others have the full complement of them. No matter which ones you currently have open, you can open to all of them by practicing the exercises in this book. Let's examine each one in depth.

The Body Sense

Our bodies are so wise, and they provide us with a very powerful (and very under-rated) psychic sense. Sometimes called the *somatic* or *kinesthetic sense,* your body is tuned to keeping you safe, and it always knows what's really happening. Just like when you turn somersaults in a pool, your body always knows which way is up; it's hard to fool this wily psychic sense. Sadly, many people ignore messages from their bodies, usually to their detriment. This is one of the reasons that I strongly recommend that psychic students learn how to stay grounded, since you will miss this rich source of psychic information if you are not actually in your body and paying attention to it.

This body sense reminds me of the hot/cold game we used to play as kids. When we get closer to something that is beneficial for us, our body will answer with pleasant physical sensations. Conversely, when we are around things that are not in our best interest or are unsafe, the body will sound the alarm. In order to listen to your body's psychic sense, you want to steer toward the pleasant sensations and away from the unpleasant ones. Just as the rudder on a ship helps you navigate through water, this body psychic sense will help steer us toward safety in the world. And let's be clear, this body sense is very much geared to your physical survival and safety, and it will always give you a message if you are in an unsafe situation—if you are paying attention.

Just as everyone's body is different, we each experience the body psychic sense differently. Pay attention to how your heart, your belly, and your skin feel and how your breathing changes. By paying attention to our unique bodies, we will find this psychic sense. Look for these types of physical sensations:

- Your heart might feel a happy, expanded warmth or a cold tightness.

- Your belly might do pleasant tummy flips when you are around someone that you really resonate with, and you might have a queasy stomach if the person is not for you.

- When our body is relaxed and safe, we will naturally slow our breathing and drop into deep belly breathing. In an unsafe situation, we will engage in shallow, rapid, chest breathing.

- Our skin is a highly sensitive organ, always tuned in to our immediate environment, so we need to take it seriously when we get excited goose-bumps or when our skin crawls.

While these sensations can also have a purely physiological cause, it takes some practice and attention to notice how your body feeds you extra psychic information. Many psychics have a very particular physical sensation that lets them know that they are getting an accurate psychic impression.

When I surveyed my psychic development class, my students reported that they felt strong sensations in their bodies when their guides were around, and when they were receiving a psychic impression. One felt full-body tingles, another felt gooseflesh. I tend to feel a strong stirring sensation at the crown of my head, almost like a fly walking through my hair. Someone else cries tears when she gets a strong psychic impression that she knows is accurate, even when she is not sad; she calls these "truth tears." This is the body's truth signal that we talked about in the previous chapter.

Jeremiah is the son of one of my close friends. He is a sensitive as well as a professional dancer and an athlete. He has learned to rely on his body's wisdom in regard to whom he can trust in his life and whom he can't. When he talked with me, Jeremiah also noted that his body psychic sense helps him feel his way through physical environments and helps him recognize when his guides are around.

✳ JEREMIAH'S STORY   *I use this all the time in my dating life. My body knows right away if my date is going to vibe with me or not, and it's not always about a sexual attraction either. I pay full attention to whether or not I want to lean in to touch someone, whether I can fully relax my belly around someone, and if I have an easy time falling asleep in someone else's presence.*

I feel an icy cold pit in my stomach if danger is around, and my mouth goes dry. I live in New York City and since I dance on Broadway, I have to take the subway home very late at night. I have to have my wits about me, but I have learned to pay attention to that sensation in my stomach since it always goes cold when danger is present. I have avoided trouble in my life since I started paying attention. The other night, I got that cold stomach and dry-mouth sensation as I was waiting for a train and took a taxi home that night instead. The next morning, the news was full of a batch of armed robberies and assaults all along that subway line.

Jeremiah is an inspiring example of someone who gets the most out of this powerful physical psychic sense. As an athlete, he has fantastic body awareness.

There are many other ways that our psychic perceptions show up in our bodies. People have reported feeling a loved one visiting from the other side touching their cheek or giving them a hug. One of my colleagues feels a warmth all through the back of her heart when her angels are around her. Clearly, there is much practical and reliable information to be had by paying attention to what our body senses.

Psychometry

Psychometry is the psychic skill of being able to receive psychic impressions by touching objects. It is a fascinating form of the body's psychic sense. I know psychics who read objects like photographs, wedding rings, watches, and eyeglasses. Anything people wear on their bodies for a long time picks up the energy of that person, and someone who does psychometry is able to read that energy.

My friend Lydia is a powerful psychic with this gift. She was drawn to working with antiques and vintage jewelry, and can often pick up psychic information about whom those objects belonged to. She says that things like watches, rings, and eyeglasses hold the strongest imprint of someone's energy, since they are items that are worn every day, sometimes for years at a time. She can tell whom the object belonged to and sense a lot of information about how that person lived and died by holding that object.

Here are some other ways to fully open up our body psychic sense.

- Take good care of your body by eating right. Many people report an increase in their psychic ability when they eat a very clean diet rich in fresh, raw, whole foods.

- Get plenty of sleep and rest. Make sure to attend to any health issues you have by seeing a doctor.

- When you meditate, pay attention to your body's sensations rather than trying to rise above them or tune them out.

- Try a physically based meditation practice like yoga, tai chi, or martial arts, or dance to increase your body awareness.

- Minimize substances that are designed to numb you out like painkillers, muscle relaxants, and excessive alcohol or drugs.

- Spend time in nature with your bare feet on the ground, and practice any other grounding techniques that you know work for you.

- Pay attention to your body's psychic signals and regularly check in with your belly and your breathing.

Your body has a beautiful array of psychic skills that can help keep you safe in the world. Your body never lies and always knows what's real and true for you. You will reap huge rewards in your psychic development if you give this body psychic sense its due.

Now let's examine a psychic sense that is closely related to this body sense. They are often connected, and many people who have the body psychic sense also have this feeling sense.

Clairsentience—The Feeling Sense

Our emotions are a powerful source of both psychic and intuitive information: this is the gift of clairsentience. Famed author and healer Anodea Judith says this in her book *Wheels of Life:* "Clairsentience is the ability to sense other people's emotions, also called empathy. This sensing does not always become information recognized by the cognitive properties of the brain. It is experienced more as a subtle feeling, as if we were experiencing the feeling ourselves."[2]

It is important to honor our feelings as a powerful psychic ability. Our emotions connect us to the right side of our brain where so many of our psychic impressions come from. Our feelings are deeply connected to our soul, and I believe that our soul speaks to us through our feelings and not so much through our thoughts. We do need our mind and its busy thoughts, of course, but many of us have grown overidentified with our thinking self and underidentified with our emotions.

"I think, therefore I am" is only part of the equation, and one of the biggest challenges that budding psychics have is learning to shift the focus of our attention from our thoughts to our feelings. Sadly, many of us have been trained to ignore and diminish our feelings and to push them away as inconvenient signs of weakness rather than to embrace the powerful psychic sense that they are. You might have a strong feeling psychic sense if you have some of these experiences:

- You are a highly emotional person and aware of your feelings throughout the day.

- You find yourself saying, "I have a good/bad feeling about that…"

- You identify yourself as an empath and can easily tune in to the physical and emotional experiences of other people.

- When you have a psychic experience, you feel it. This might be a combination of sensations and emotions.

- You feel the presence of spirits around you, and you probably also know what they are feeling.

- You feel and sense energy too, whether it's from people or the energy of the environments that you occupy.

Soul Feelings vs. Reactive Feelings

One of the most important things to do as a clairsentient is to deeply understand our own feelings. Our feelings are a mix of our emotional states combined with sensations in our body to which our feelings are connected. For our purposes of psychic development, I make a distinction between two different types of feelings: soul feelings and reactive feelings.

Soul feelings arise in the moment in response to whatever situation we are in. If you look at really small children, you will see them go through their soul feelings all day long. When they feel something, they express it right then and there in the moment without worrying about it or talking themselves out of it. When they are sad, they cry; when they are happy, they laugh; and when they are angry, we all know about it!

As we grow up, we learn to disconnect from our emotions as they arise, to stuff them and shove them down. In order to benefit from the intuitive and psychic guidance of our emotions, we must allow ourselves to feel our soul feelings. We will talk about how to do this at the end of this section.

In contrast to our soul feelings, we also have *reactive feelings*. These emotions generally stem from past, unhealed traumas. They overtake us, pull us out of the present moment, and trap us into reacting based on something from the past. Anxiety is a great example of a reactive emotion, whereas fear is a soul emotion.

Fear is an appropriate response to actual danger and might save your life by activating your fight/flight response. When we feel anxiety, on the other hand, we anticipate that something bad will or might happen in the future, even though it isn't actually happening at the moment.

While there is a sweetness about soul feelings, reactive emotions just feel bad. Alongside anxiety, they might include feelings like jealousy, rage, numbness, hurt, and hatred. Reactive emotions filter up through unhealed trauma. They are guiding you to heal the trauma, but they are not part of your psychic senses.

A reactive feeling is more like a knee-jerk response, a flash-in-the-pan emotional moment, based on our impulses and instincts. You might, for example, have the impulse to rage and lash out in anger if someone cuts you off in traffic. Reactive feelings are triggered by our nervous system and our fight-or-flight mechanism. They are hormone driven and chemical in nature, like the flush of adrenaline that floods our system when someone cuts us off. Your autonomic nervous system reacts to potential danger, and it signals your adrenal glands to dump a lot of cortisol and adrenaline into your blood stream so you can fight or flee and deal with the danger. In that adrenaline-fueled haze, you have an impulse to lash out and punch someone, or even maybe feel a momentary desire to kill them.

Once the adrenaline clears out of your system about twenty minutes later, that impulse is gone and you go back to being a peace-loving person who would never hurt or kill anyone. If you feel triggered, aggressive, hostile, or anxious, it's a usually a reactive emotion. The feeling washing over you is a mix of hormones, nervous system reactions, and unhealed past traumas. It leaves you feeling unbalanced and unlike yourself—until the chemical fog clears and you feel like yourself again.

Soul feelings, while they can be intense, tend to endure for longer than a few minutes, and they come from a deep place within us. They arise from our soul, and their purpose is to guide us to live a more authentic life. Even tough soul feelings, such as deep grief, have a sweetness and authenticity to them. We grieve because we have loved deeply. Soul feelings are inspiring, leading us to want to express them in creative ways. Poets, songwriters, and artists capture these soul feelings in their works of art.

An example of this that we can all relate to is the difference between the true feeling of love versus the reactive experience of infatuation. The soul feeling of love is enduring, while infatuation and lust don't last and contain a lot of nervous system excitation and hormone-driven desire.

Your soul feelings are part of your psychic senses, but your reactive feelings are not. So as we open up this psychic sense, we need to distinguish between the two. In short, if you are triggered and reactive, it's not a psychic impression. However, our soul feelings give us constant psychic feedback.

Let's add on another layer here. If one of your primary psychic senses is your feelings, chances are very good that you are also an empath. That means that we have to contend with other people's emotional states as well as our own.

The Psychic Gift of the Empath

Empaths are the psychic sponges of the world, and to be empathic is its own unique psychic gift. Empaths literally absorb the sensations, emotions, thoughts, and energy of other people. We run this energy through our own system in a way that makes us feel like the energy of others is actually our energy that we are feeling.

On our good days, we are natural healers, helpers, and caretakers. We use this psychic sense to help us understand how other people are doing, even when they can't communicate it directly to us. We know because we feel their experience as if it were our own. On our bad days, we are an emotional hot mess, flooded with other people's energetic and emotional goo, and unable to tell the difference between our own experience and someone else's.

Empathy is the gift of the healer, and most empaths that I have worked with are wired that way because their life purpose is to be a healer or helper in some way. It's a beautiful gift! Empaths need help learning to manage their energy so they can be comfortable in the world.

Am I an Empath?

Do you wonder if you might be an empath? Here are some experiences that are common to all empaths:

⊛ You feel what other people feel as if it were your own feelings. This can also include physical sensations and thoughts.

⊛ You are deeply emotional yourself, and people tell you that you are too sensitive.

⊛ You are highly tuned to your environments. Some places feel good, and other places feel not so good.

⊛ You are introverted and big crowds of people can make you uncomfortable. It's easier for you to be one-on-one with people.

⊛ Lots of noise, lights, and other stimulation swamps your nervous system, so a big box store leaves you feeling limp.

⊛ You are drawn to animals, plants, and small children.

> ✸ You feel the presence of spirits around you, and you probably know what those spirits are feeling.
>
> Being an empath certainly has its challenges, but it's a very powerful psychic skill that can be hugely beneficial when we learn how to manage the intensity of our own feelings and how to filter out the static of the world and other people's feelings.

Let's take a look at how being an empath is really a psychic gift. Recently, I worked with a young empath named Kristie. She came to my office for some healing sessions after having read my book *Energy Healing for Empaths*. She needed help learning how to handle the psychic overload she was experiencing as a college student. Kristie was having a textbook empath experience and in a tough environment too. She was in a big university and lived in a crowded dorm on a busy campus, with lots of drama and emotions flying all over the place. Kristie explained to me that she was also the unofficial counselor and healer in her friend group.

✷ KRISTIE'S STORY   *I thought I would love college, but I was a big emotional hot mess, feeling anxious and depressed. Sometimes I get migraines or stomachaches that are so bad that I can't go to classes. Everyone tells me that I am too sensitive and that I need to get a thicker skin, but I just end up feeling everyone's stuff. Everyone comes to me with their problems and issues, and I end up taking care of everyone.*

Also, my dorm is rather haunted, and I can feel the presence of spirits there. I don't see anything, I just feel them. I sense that they are there, and I know how the spirits are feeling too. There is one lounge that no one ever goes into because of the sad ghost that hangs out there.

In Kristie's story, you can see so many of the psychic gifts that empaths share. As we worked together, she found that her skills as an empath were part of her psychic gifts. Once she learned to manage her energy better using the grounding, clearing, and protecting exercises, life in the dorm was easier for her, and her health issues—her depression and anxiety—eased up. She found the skills of turning her psychic abilities off particularly helpful and used the space-clearing protocol to rid her dorm of spirits and leftover residual energy. She was also able to see that these gifts were actually part of her life's purpose to be a healer, and she studied to be a counselor.

Empaths have three very strong psychic skills: physical empathy, emotional empathy, and sometimes telepathy. Let's take a closer look at each of these skills.

Physical Empathy. When we feel in our own body what someone else is feeling in their body, we're experiencing physical empathy. It might be as simple as sitting next to someone who has a headache and then suddenly our own head starts hurting. It can also happen to people whom we are emotionally close to even if they are not physically present with us. Physical empathy is a fantastic source of psychic information designed to help us understand how someone else is feeling in their body, even if they can't express it themselves.

Emotional Empathy. Empaths feel other people's emotions as if they are their own. It's deeper than just noticing what someone is feeling. Empaths literally absorb the emotional energy of others and run that energy through their own systems. We feel what others feel as if that feeling was our own. This psychic gift can help us assess other people's emotional states.

Telepathy/Thought Reading. Many empaths can read the thoughts of others, which can be a disconcerting experience. For me, it was like hearing someone's thinking as if they had spoken out loud. When I was younger, I would often ask people if they had said something, when I was really just hearing their thoughts as if they had spoken out loud. We will discuss this more in depth when we cover the auditory psychic ability in the next section.

There is a strong connection between being clairsentient and being an empath. The difference might be that clairsentients have advanced the empath's skills to the point where they are achieving great psychic insights based on what they are feeling.

PSYCHIC TIP: *Is This Mine?*

If you are an empath, one of the most important skills that you need to learn is to distinguish between your own emotions, energy, body sensations, and thoughts and those of others. When you are feeling something, ask yourself, *Is this mine?* With practice, you will soon be able to tell what is yours and what isn't, since you will feel, know, or sense that it is or isn't yours. You can use your pendulum to check if you are still not sure, or try journaling it out. If it's not yours, release it using the grounding and clearing practices that you learned in chapter 2.

The feeling psychic sense is a powerful and useful one. It is often the primary psychic sense for empaths. If you are an empath, your emotions are your superpower as is your ability to read the emotional states of others. I urge you not to dismiss this psychic sense as less than any of the other ones.

My friend Amy is one of the most powerful healers that I know. Here is what she said about her struggle to realize how psychic she really is.

❋ AMY'S STORY   I never saw myself as being psychic at all. And to be honest, I didn't even think I was psychic when I became an energy healer. I always secretly felt bad about this part of myself, because I don't often see things the way most psychics and healers do. I will never forget the moment many years ago when I learned that I just process the world differently than others, and that my ability to feel everything very deeply allows me to sense, feel, and know things that other people may not even be aware of—and that this is how I receive psychic information.

For most of my life, this made me feel like I was crazy. It took a lot of inner work to accept this part of myself, since I had been rejected by others for so long because of it. As a result, I then rejected these parts of myself. I could see that I really was psychic and that all that sensitivity was a gift meant to help other people. Then I realized that my ability to feel things deeply no longer felt like the curse I once thought it was, but it was actually my greatest spiritual gift. My life finally made perfect sense as everything fell right into place for the first time ever.

To take advantage of this psychic sense, we need some retraining to attend to and value our emotional states. If you want to expand this psychic sense, commit to a daily practice of monitoring and expressing your feelings so that you are always paying attention to how you feel.

Tips for a Clairsentience Practice

In order to tell the difference between true or soul feelings and reactive feelings, we need to pay close attention to our feelings on a regular basis. Keeping track of our feelings on a daily basis can help us learn to distinguish between the soulful true feelings and the impulsive reactive feelings. When we do that, we can notice what messages our true feelings are sending us.

- Journaling and meditation are both easy and effective ways to pay attention to and clear out your feelings.

- Try some healing modalities like Reiki or EFT (emotional freedom technique). You can do Reiki on yourself to help you process your feelings.

- If you have a lot of reactive feelings due to emotional trauma, get some counseling and do trauma recovery work with a professional.

- If you are an empath, practice the daily energy management exercises to ground, clear, and protect yourself.

We have fully explored the feeling psychic sense or clairsentience. Now let's move on to the knowing psychic sense, also known as claircognizance.

Claircognizance—The Knowing Sense

If you have ever said to yourself, *I don't know why I know, I just do!* you have this psychic sense. If so, congratulations, since it is a very accurate, useful, and highly reliable psychic sense. It's something that we feel in our gut, an inner knowing that sometimes defies our mental knowing.

Back in the day, it used to be called "mother's intuition," and many of us knew that there was no fooling our mothers who seemed to have the same psychic knowledge as the Oracle at Delphi. Our mothers knew when we lied about brushing our teeth, when we skipped band practice to smoke in the woods with our pals, or when we let the dog eat our homework on purpose.

The knowing psychic sense arises out of our gut, and many people report feeling strong sensations in their belly when they get psychic messages through this channel. Much of this psychic sense is based on a kind of threat assessment. Many people, especially if they have a little bit of a warrior spirit in them, send out energetic feelers from their solar plexus like a kind of psychic sonar. This is how they—and we—"read the room" and everyone in it. This knowing psychic sense is looking for dangerous people and tends to categorize people as good, bad, and neutral within about ten seconds of meeting them.

It's so interesting that these days doctors are calling the gut the "second brain" since research suggests that our intuition has a real and measurable presence in our guts. The gut is lined with a network of millions of neurons, in a system called the "enteric nervous system." The gut has more neurons than the spinal cord, and this research helps us to understand why we really do think with our gut.

Here are the other characteristics of being claircognizant:

- You feel things in your gut, in that "I just know" way.

- You might know things and not be sure why or how you know them. One of my friends could beat everyone at trivia and often never knew how she knew things.

- You are an excellent judge of character and know when people are lying or not being authentic.

- You scan the room subconsciously, looking for danger or who needs help.

- Your psychic information often comes in the form of hunches or nudges.

- You are practical and have strong common sense.

- You are very good at problem solving, and you do it in a practical way where the answers just pop into your mind as you see how things fit together.

- You have a logical, strategic way of thinking, almost like a chess player, and you can see many moves down the road.

- You know about things long before they actually happen, so it's really hard to surprise you.

If you find that you have a natural gift for this, then congratulations. Claircognizance is a very solid, practical, and reliable psychic sense.

Your Gut vs. Your Mind

For most people with a strong claircognizance, the biggest struggle that they have is the continual argument between the mind and the gut knowing. They both have a kind of logic to them, but they can be on very different pages and tuned in to different ways of experiencing the world. Your mind experiences the world in a way that is based on your beliefs, your social conditioning, and your ideologies, whereas your gut may bypass all of that and come up with a very direct and immediate judgment.

For example, your mind might really believe that "good people" try to like everyone, so you are not going to make snap evaluations about people or situations. However, your gut may well make a snap judgment about someone you meet, since that is one of the superpowers of people who are claircognizant. This can mean that our minds and our gut argue frequently about what is really happening. Here is an example of what often happens in this gut versus mind conflict when you meet a new person.

Your Mind: That is a nice person. I am glad we met.

Your Gut: Really? I don't trust them. In fact, they give me the willies. They have weird and icky energy. Something is really off there.

Your Mind: What is wrong with you? Everyone else likes them. We are going to give them a chance.

Your Gut: Okay, but when it all goes bad, I'll be saying, "I told you so…"

We have all had this inner conversation, and we know what happens when we don't trust our gut. Our minds are actually not very psychic, and the analysis part of us misses all of the subtle clues that allow our gut to know the truth.

Tips for a Claircognizance Practice

The number one thing we can do to open up our psychic sense of knowing is to pay attention when we feel that nudge. Here are a few other tips:

- Write down your hits in your journal so you don't forget them. You might know something is going to happen on a Monday and then, unless you record it somewhere, you forget about it totally. When it does happen a few days later, you can claim psychic brownie points for knowing that it was going to happen. Recording hits in your journal trains you to pay attention and remember your inner knowings.

- Learn to trust your gut by remembering that if it's anxiety, it's going to feel bad like all reactive feelings do. A real intuitive hit feels neutral, even if it's about something intense.

- By paying attention to your inner knowing, you will soon learn to distinguish the difference between your mind and your gut knowing.

- Act on your knowings at least most of the time. Getting a knowing and then not acting on it is a sure way to shut it down. It doesn't mean you need to carry out every one, but more often than not, it's a good way to put your money where your mouth is.

- Pay attention to your sense of integrity. Your personal moral compass is closely connected with your gut knowing. Your gut will tell you if you have veered off from your own integrity, and it will constantly ping you to help you notice and align with your own integrity. If you constantly go against your own integrity, your inner knowing will shut down.

Intuition: Body, Feeling, and Knowing Come Together

Our intuition is made up of these three psychic senses—the body sense, the feeling sense, and the knowing sense—when they all come together. The knowing sense is like the brain of our gut, and it organizes the body psychic sense and our feeling sense into a laser-like knowing. Since they make up the backbone of our intuition, many people have all three of these psychic senses. If you fall into that category, then it's really important to notice when all three of these psychic senses are in agreement with each other. That is a sure sign that your intuition is active. In these cases, you can count on your intuitive realizations to be correct. If you don't have a fully activated set of senses yet, it's easy to develop them.

PSYCHIC TIP: *Breathing to Open Your Intuition*

To tune in to your gut knowing, relax your diaphragm and slow down your breathing. When we tighten our diaphragm and breathe shallowly from the upper chest, we tend to cut ourselves off from our intuition and deeper knowing. This is how we breathe when we are feeling emotionally reactive. Try a few centering breaths, relax your belly, and let your breath drop deep into your lower belly. Then tune in to what your gut is telling you.

Now we are going to explore two of the stranger psychic senses, those of smell and taste. You may never have heard of clairalience and clairgustance, but it's important to know that they exist and how they manifest themselves.

Clairalience and Clairgustance: The Smell and Taste Senses

These skills are somewhat rarer than the other ones that we have been talking about, but they are fascinating and worth discussing. These are the ability to perceive smells (*clairalience*) and tastes (*clairgustance*) that have no physical source but rather emanate from the spirit world. You might, for example, experience the scent of perfume, flowers, or cigarette smoke.

We connect these psychic senses of smell and taste since they are often connected in our physical senses too. For example, one of my clients had a strong connection to her grandmother, who had loved to cook for her family, and she could smell and taste the Italian cookies called pizzelles whenever the spirit of her beloved nonna was around.

I have smelled wood smoke and tasted ashes in a brand-new home. It was built on top of a house that burned down over fifty years ago. It was like the psychic imprint of the fire was still there, and the smell and taste of it were a part of that psychic imprint.

Our sense of smell is very closely linked with our memory, and sometimes odors can take us back in time like nothing else can. I don't get too many spirit visitations from my grandmother, but when I do, I always know she is there because I can smell the inside of her purse. It smells like lavender, spearmint gum, money, and the perfume she always wore. There is no other smell like it, and it takes me back to earlier days every time I smell it. I know it's her because of that smell.

This psychic sense often comes to people who have strong mediumship abilities. *Mediums* are psychics who specialize in communicating with those who have passed away. Many mediums report that they know a spirit is around them because they suddenly can smell and taste something, which can be a powerful and undeniable signal to the living people that their deceased loved one is truly present.

My friend Rosario is a powerful and popular medium. She recounted this about a recent mediumship session she did.

✴ ROSARIO'S STORY   *I just did a mediumship session for a large family who had lost their father. He was the patriarch of a large clan, and he had died very suddenly and without a will. There was a lot of tension among the family members and about ten of them crowded into my office.*

There was a dispute over money and property and how his remains should be honored. Everyone was squabbling when all of the sudden, we could all smell such a strong odor of cigar smoke, whiskey, and strong cologne, like Old Spice. It was so clear, so pungent that everyone stopped talking all at once. It was Pappa, there was no doubt about it. He had some very direct messages to deliver, in Spanish, which fortunately, I speak pretty well.

This was such a clear sign that he was present that it cut through the discord and quieted the skeptics, who now had no doubt that he was really there. The smell was so thick that we had to open a window, and it lingered for a while after the family left. It made the session so much easier for me, since they all snapped to attention to do his wishes, and I felt that he was pleased with the outcome.

Sometimes our spirit guides will let us know that they are around through odors. It is said that saints like Mother Mary and Saint Thérèse of Lisieux announce themselves with the fragrance of roses. And mystics throughout the ages have reported that angels, saints, and other holy beings bring with their visitations a beautiful and indescribable perfume called the *odor of sanctity*. There are also some negative entities that announce their presence through odors like dampness, dirt, and rot in the classic graveyard smell, and even more unpleasant odors.

Some psychics report being able to smell energy too. This is a kind of *synesthesia*, where our senses combine. With synesthesia, people can hear or even smell colors, for example. I know healers who can smell cancer in someone. Recent scientific studies have documented that dogs can easily smell cancer, because it really does have a distinguishable scent. As a psychic, you might also say something like you "smell a rat" or that something "smells off" when you are picking up energy with this psychic sense.

You may well have the psychic senses of taste and smell if you have experiences like these:

- You have a very sensitive sense of taste and smell.

- You smell or taste something that isn't there, especially if it comes with a spirit visitation from a loved one.

- This smell/taste combo brings back a strong memory for you that helps you identify a spirit.

- You have latent mediumship abilities and can connect with the spirits of the dead.

- You can smell trouble brewing or smell it when the wind shifts in your favor.

I love this psychic sense set and encourage you to pay attention to it as we move through the exercises in this book to see if you also possess it. I am convinced that whatever psychic perceptions we have will grow stronger and more accurate with our attention and with persistent practice, so let's all try to boost these two enticing psychic senses. Now let's move on to the psychic sense of hearing.

Clairaudience—The Auditory Sense

Clairaudience is the ability to hear psychic information. While sometimes this does happen with our physical ears, it is mostly likely to be happening with our psychic ears. The auditory psychic sense is very common and also highly useful once we learn to master it. It can bring up some fear for people who have it, since in the past, hearing voices in your head could land you in a psychiatric facility. People who are clairaudient are auditory learners, have acute hearing, and are often very attracted to music. Clairaudients make great phone psychics!

You have the gift of clairaudience if you

- have an acute sense of hearing and a logical mind,

- have an affinity for music, either listening to it or playing it yourself,

- easily express yourself by speaking and you are a good listener,

- are aware of your inner voice and are often talking to yourself in your own head,

- sometimes say something extra cool that might not be you,

- hear footsteps or other noises when no one else is around,

- hear ringing or buzzing in your ears, and

- can really connect to someone by talking to them, even on the phone.

Your Inner Voice vs. Clairaudience

The most difficult part of this psychic skill comes in learning to tell the difference between your own inner voice and the voices of your guides. Because I have always been aware of my inner voice, I was shocked to learn that not everyone has one. Listening to and talking with your inner voice is like having a constant conversation with yourself in your head. For me, the inner voice is the one that talks in circles and has a rather predictable script to it.

Mine sounds sort of like this: *Let's see, if I get this chapter done by this evening, I will have time to go to my favorite restaurant for dinner. Wait…are they open on Mondays? I can't remember. But I bet my sister knows. Should I text her, or just look it up?* Sometimes it really is that banal. And sometimes it's deep and insightful. Whether it's banal or insightful, that inner voice is pretty constant.

When I was young and studying with one of my first psychic teachers, she had us do an exercise to see if we could track this inner monologue. The exercise required stopping and noticing the inner voice throughout the day. We kept track of our inner conversations in a journal, just for a week or two. During that time, I began to notice that sometimes the voice in my head had a different quality to it. I became aware of the pattern that I had of inner speaking, which was a looping around and rather circular, like a meandering stream of consciousness. While this other voice, the voice of my guide, was strong, directive, and very much to the point. When that voice comes in, it cuts like a knife through my internal chatter; it is, in fact, rather bossy. My guides often cut across my own inner blarney with a very important message for me:

Pay attention now, something important is happening.

Don't talk, just listen.

Or one time when I was having an argument with my partner:

He's right, you know. Swallow your pride and see if you can see his point.

I knew this wasn't my own voice, since I was sure I was right! Over time, I have come to fully trust this other voice. Even if sometimes the truth hurts, I appreciate the reminders and the different perspective. Often the voice of your guides has a different sound quality than your own. It could be deeper, louder, softer, and more melodic than your own voice, so that it literally sounds different than your own inner voice. One of my students has a guide that speaks in rhyme, and another student has a guide with a strong Irish brogue that is not something she can replicate on her own.

Channeling

Some psychics are *channels*—they have an ability to speak or write messages that come directly from their guides. If you are a channel, this is an important part of your life purpose and is usually an agreement between you and your guides. These types of psychics always have clairaudience as one if their strong psychic skills. Esther Hicks, Edgar Cayce, Paul Selig, Lee Harris, and many other famous psychics report that they are an instrument that the spiritual beings speak through with the purpose of relaying information to the pubic or to individual clients. This can be related to the idea of the muse that many writers, poets, and musicians say inspires and drives their creativity.

Jaslene is sweet-natured Reiki practitioner that I met at one of my Reiki classes. She has a loving, compassionate heart and is a very successful Reiki practitioner. She volunteers to give Reiki sessions in nursing homes and hospitals, and whenever I see her, she has a big blue angel standing right behind her. She told me that her angel communicates with her by working through her feeling and auditory psychic senses.

✳ JASLENE'S STORY   *I just get a feeling that I am supposed to go somewhere, and I don't know why. Just the other day, I was in the hospital, and I got that feeling that I should go to the cafeteria and get a cup of tea. I didn't really want one, but these days, I just go with the flow.*

Once I was there, I saw a young girl crying in the checkout line. She didn't have enough money for lunch, so I paid for her lunch and we talked for a while. Turns out she had just lost her mother and was feeling at her wits' end, like maybe life wasn't worth living anymore. We talked for a while, and then I felt a tingle in my throat and heart. When I feel that, I know that the angel wants to say something through me, so I said some things that she needed to hear. I know it was my angel directing me to be where I needed to be and say what needed to be said.

Jaslene is an inspiration. She's an example of what can happen when we trust our guidance and allow the full gift of clairaudience to work through us.

PSYCHIC TIP: *Automatic Writing*

This is a great way to develop the gift of clairaudience. To do this, you can write longhand or on your computer. Start by doing a ground, clear, and protect meditation. You can also call in specific guides, if you know who you want to connect with. Then write down a question and without thinking about the answer too much, just start writing it. If you relax and go with the flow, it's a great way to build up your clairaudience since you will soon begin to really hear the voices of your guides.

Up next we have clairvoyance, the visual psychic sense. This one is tricky to have because it's the one that has the most mythos around it due to what we see in the media about psychics. Let's jump in and find out the truth about this psychic sense.

Clairvoyance: The Visual Sense

Clairvoyance is the ability to see and visualize the nonordinary and nonphysical worlds. Clairvoyants perceive this in a visual way, most of the time by seeing things with the inner, psychic eye, but sometimes seeing things with their physical eyes.

For most visual psychics, it's like watching a little movie in their head. This can happen at any time, including when meditating or daydreaming. Many clairvoyants see colors around people, have intense and vivid dreams, and sometimes see things out of the corner of their eyes. It's our peripheral vision that is the most psychically aware. When we look at things directly, we are more likely to be in a beta brain wave, so the information goes to our cognitive mind.

In contrast to this, we are more apt to see the nonordinary worlds when we use our peripheral vision. We might see spiritual beings, energy around people and places, as well as seeing the past and the future. We have the ability to see it all, the good and the bad, and somehow seeing things makes it all more real.

This is a fascinating and, at times, challenging psychic skill. Here are some ways to tell if you have it:

- You have a strong imagination and the ability to visualize easily.

- You have vivid dreams, and it's easy for you to remember them. You might even have lucid dreams, which is when we are aware that we are dreaming while we are still asleep.

- Sometimes you see something out of the corner of your eye, and when you turn your head to look at it directly, nothing is there.

- You see energy and colors around people or even objects. This might be pops and flashes of light, patches of color, or a shimmery heat-like distortion.

- Psychic information comes to you like flashes of a vision or a little movie running through your mind.

- When spirits are around, you see them in your mind's eye or even see them as if they are physical.

- You have a deep love of the visual arts.

Visual psychics frequently get their information through dreams. We will discuss how to work with our dreams in chapter 4.

Psychic seeing is a double-edged sword. It's one of the rarer psychic senses, and yet the media would tell us it's the *only* kind of psychic experience. This leads many highly psychic people to dismiss their own gifts because they are not visual psychics. Somehow clairvoyance has become synonymous with being psychic.

And yet, most people who have a strong visual psychic gift struggle with it. It's not an easy one to have, and my psychic development classes are full of people who are looking for ways to turn it off, much as I did when I was younger.

Seeing the Truth

Being clairvoyant is more than seeing psychic visions. A big part of the gift is the ability to actually see what's real; it's seeing the truth. Let me define what I mean by "real." When it's open, our third eye is meant to take in actual reality, to see what is really there in the world and to witness it without making things up or seeing things through the filters of our minds.

What most people do is take the stories that are in their own head and then project those out onto the world. As a result, they are perceiving a version of reality based on their own beliefs, ideas, and judgments, most of which arise out of their unconscious programming. They see the world through a series of filters that curate their experience, and yet they think it's "real." For example, you might believe what you have been told about who the "good" and "bad" people are based on the outer trappings of those people, like where they live, what they look like, and how much money they make.

People with clairvoyance tend to see beyond the surface and look at the deeper levels of reality, like the character of someone's heart and soul over their appearance.

True clairvoyants see the world with far fewer filters. It's very much like the story "The Emperor's New Clothes": there is only one person in the crowd who can see and acknowledge the truth that the emperor has no clothes on at all. He sees reality, but everyone else thinks he's crazy. This is what is truly difficult about being clairvoyant. You could be the one person in a room of a hundred people who sees the truth, so it's often an isolating experience. True clairvoyants will find themselves saying, "How can I be the only person that is seeing this?" when we see the shenanigans at the office or within our own families.

Often this person is rejected or vilified by others, and it can be really difficult if you also choose to speak the truths that you are seeing. Clairvoyants tend to make other people uncomfortable as we can see through the facades that they project. I often think about Dorothy from *The Wizard of Oz*, who is a great example of a clairvoyant. She can see the truth of who everyone really is, especially when they get to the "Don't look at the man behind the curtain!" moment of the movie. Clairvoyants always see the man behind the curtain.

If you have this aspect of the visual psychic ability, it's important to learn discernment. Using your intuition can help you decide when, where, and how to speak your truth.

The bottom line here is that clairvoyance has two aspects to it. One is the ability to see visions, spirits, and energy as our primary psychic sense. The other is the ability to see the truth, not so much from a psychic vision standpoint, but to see the truth inside the illusions that many people present. And although this a powerful psychic sense to have, it's not always the easiest.

Let's talk about what your third eye really is. Then we'll learn how to open it up even more.

The Third Eye and the Pineal Gland

The visual psychic skill is often referred to as the *third eye*, and it is a very accurate name for it. This concept of the third eye is associated to your pineal gland, which is a small almond-shaped endocrine gland right in the center of your brain, behind your forehead. It produces melatonin and helps regulate our sleep cycle. It also produces DMT, which is responsible for some of our peak spiritual experiences, including psychic visions. Interestingly enough, the pineal gland is also full of optic nerves, so it really is like another eye.

Tips for Opening the Pineal Gland

There are many things to do to open up and activate our pineal glands. Here are a few:

⊛ Meditation is the best way. Try pulling your breath up from the base of your spine to the center of your forehead.

⊛ Spend time in the sun without your sunglasses on; sunlight is a strong activating force for your pineal gland. (Please don't look directly at the sun, which can harm your vision.) Minimize your exposure to the chemicals of chlorine, fluoride, and bromine, which are known to shut down the pineal gland. Fluoride is a common ingredient in toothpaste, and all three of these chemicals can be found in treated tap water.

⊛ Sandalwood is a great opener for this gland. Sandalwood incense or essential oil applied to the forehead can open the gland up, or try burning sandalwood incense when you meditate.

⊛ Crystals like amethyst and sodalite are also helpful. Sleeping with an amethyst crystal under your pillow can help you remember your dreams and have more psychic dreams. You can also gaze into or hold an amethyst crystal when you meditate to help you open your psychic vision.

Mystics have long known that stimulating this gland through meditation and spiritual practices opens us up to more psychic and spiritual experiences, so this part of our brain has been called the "seat of the soul." When we open and activate the pineal gland, we can increase our psychic vision.

Many visual psychics complain of feeling overwhelmed and overstimulated by this psychic sense. It's not so much about trying to open it up as it is about shutting it down when you have had enough. We must be a little mindful about what visual stimulation we engage with. Scary movies or TV shows filled with violence can blow our circuits, so please be careful about what you are visually consuming if you have this psychic sense. You might consider putting yourself on a strict media diet. Spending time in nature or a museum and looking at beauty can be a great antidote to all of the terrible things we end up seeing in the world.

PSYCHIC TIP: *Clearing Your Third Eye*

If your visual psychic sense is overly open and you need help closing it down, try putting your hand on your forehead and breathing deeply. Exhale any images that you are holding on to down the grounding cord. Send energy from the palm of your hand into your third eye to calm and soothe it. Suggest to yourself that it's okay to temporarily shut down your psychic vision so you can relax. Say to yourself, *Calm, clear, and relax now…*

Now let's take a look at the specialties of mediumship and precognition. These are not exactly psychic senses, but they are strong psychic gifts that can be experienced through any and all of our psychic senses.

The Psychic Skill of Mediumship

Mediums are psychics that specialize in communicating with the spirits of those who have passed away. These perceptions might come through any and all of your open psychic channels, so some people see the dead, hear them, feel them, sense them, or just know that they are around. Some people use the words "psychic" and "medium" interchangeably, but mediumship is really a subset under the broader term psychic. I know plenty of psychics who are not mediums and also some mediums that don't have any other psychic skills.

Visiting with a medium is an incredibly healing experience for people who have lost a loved one. Mediums can provide closure by delivering messages between the living and the dead, and they assist the souls of the departed with their transition to the other side, which isn't always so easy. Sometimes these souls get stuck and can't cross over, which is what we would call a ghost. Mediums also help the living process their loss too. Sometimes this gift is something that you are born with, and other times it comes as the result of a trauma, like a concussion or a near-death experience.

All of this requires specialized training, but it's a gift worth cultivating if you feel called to it. It's a beautiful and needed gift, and if you have this, I want to take a moment to honor you and thank you for the work that you are doing in the world. You may well have the gift of mediumship if you

- perceive around you the presence of those that have passed,

- feel like you are a ghost magnet, attracting spirits to you no matter where you go,

- sense when someone is going to die before it happens, and

- feel drawn to working with people either at their birth or their death.

We will discuss this fascinating topic at length in chapter 9. Among other things, we'll explore what happens when you die, why some people get stuck, and how to help someone cross over.

Precognition: Perceiving the Future

Precognition, also known as *prescience*, is the ability to sense the future, and like mediumship, we can perceive this through any of our open channels. This is one of the most common psychic gifts, and many people report having the foreknowing of an event.

The best analogy that I have for this is to imagine that we are like a spider sitting at the center of a web. This web stretches out all around us, including into the past and the future. When something big is about to happen, it tickles the outside edge of the web and we feel it before it quite happens. And that is why people sometimes refer to this gift as their "spider sense."

Certain events create a kind of disturbance in the force, if you will allow me a Stars Wars analogy. The upcoming death or birth of someone in our circle is one of the most common precognitive experiences. The *death bed visitation* is the single most reported psychic experience. This is when someone who has very recently passed away comes to visit and say good-bye to their loved ones. We might see them in a dream, but it can also be a knowing, or waking up in the middle of the night to perceive your loved one standing in the room only to find out that they have already passed away.

> ## PSYCHIC TIP: *Perceiving and Experiencing vs. "Seeing"*
>
> As we go forward from here, I want to invite you to change your vocabulary. Move away from the idea of "seeing" things to perceiving or experiencing psychic phenomenon. As we go through the exercises in the book, you might perceive tons of things and dismiss them all if you are not actually seeing them. Sometimes the students in my psychic development classes say, "I didn't see anything!" But if I ask, "Well, what did you experience?" they suddenly have a lot to report. The words "perceiving" and "experiencing" open us to examine all our different psychic senses.

Delusions vs. Psychic Experiences

How do we tell the difference between a real psychic hit and something that is a delusion? I always say that there are only a few letters difference between psychic and psychotic, and it can be a very difficult distinction to make. Highly psychic people who have unhealed trauma and/or mental health issues can experience psychic impressions through the lens of their mental health issues, which distort the psychic impressions into delusions.

We may think of our psychic experiences as coming through our third eye. When that lens is cracked due to a mental health condition or through unhealed trauma, we might see our angels as demons or project our trauma out into the world as psychosis.

It is important to realize that hearing voices and seeing things may be psychic impressions, or it might be a sign of mental illness. The big difference is the amount of distress these messages bring you and the amount of control you have over them.

If the voices or visions are intrusive, create more anxiety than you can handle, or happen without your control, or if they are telling you to harm yourself or others, it is vital that you seek help from a psychiatric or medical professional or go to your nearest emergency room for a psychiatric evaluation. People with strong psychic abilities still have the ability to control their psychic experiences and moderate their experiences with their spirit guides. People who are in the grips of a mental illness can't control these experiences and they can turn dark very quickly.

Sometimes people in your life who are doubters or very fearful of your gifts might try to tell you that you are delusional when you aren't. And sometimes they might give you feedback that your experiences are not normal even for psychics. If you feel like your psychic experiences are out of control, it's time to seek an experienced and trusted second opinion.

Psychic development is not recommended for people who are actively struggling with their mental health. If you are on shaky ground with your mental health, focus on getting expert help and support, and work on your energy management fundamentals before you do any further psychic development.

What's Next?

I hope that you now have a solid idea of what your psychic senses are and how to develop them even further. Next, let's discover how to use dreams, signs, and omens to help you exercise your psychic muscles and get even more confirmation on your psychic hits.

Chapter 4

Mine Dreams, Signs, and Omens for Information

We can ramp up our psychic skills considerably and have a lot of fun by using divination tools, such as oracle cards, as well as learning to interpret our dreams. Our world is alive with signs and omens that can help us confirm our psychic messages—once we learn to mine these rich sources of psychic information. However, all of these things start with our ability to understand their symbolism.

Learning the Language of Symbols

One of the most challenging skills for psychic students to attain is the ability to decode the psychic messages that we receive. Sometimes our psychic information is clear as a bell, and sometimes it arrives in the more cryptic language of symbols and metaphors. While half of our mind is wired for logical and linear thinking, our psychic downloads come to the other part of our mind, this right-brained side of us, which is all about symbolic thinking. Learning to understand the language of symbols is key, since all psychic students will have the experience of receiving a clear message but also need to be able to puzzle out what it really means.

As a young, newbie psychic, I had an experience with a client that changed the way that I did my readings. I was working at a psychic fair, doing mini-sessions as part of my psychic training. My client was a young woman who had no particular question to ask me but rather just wanted to know what I would pick up on my own. She said something like "Just tell me what I need to hear today."

She sat in a chair while I stood behind her with my hands on her shoulders. I opened myself up in that blank, receptive state and perceived something that I could not make sense of—a bowl of tangerines. It was a very vivid perception: I could smell the tangerines, and see their little pitted skin. I could taste them too—it was as if all of my senses were flooded with the experience of tangerines. On a wooden table, I could see the wooden bowl in which the tangerines sat. I felt sunshine on my skin—it was a warm summer day outside. And I felt unbearably sad too.

I thought to myself, *Yikes, what the heck does this mean? A bowl of tangerines? I can't possibly say this out loud, it's nuts. What does that even mean?* And I briefly went down the rabbit hole of doubt, questioning what I was seeing, but my teacher had been encouraging us to say what we perceived without judging or interpreting. So I took the plunge and told my client about it. I included all the details, and much to my surprise, she burst into tears.

"I was ten years old when my mother died," she told me. "I was sitting at my grandmother's kitchen table when my father came in and told me that she was gone. There was a wooden bowl full of tangerines on the kitchen table, and I remember holding one in my hand as I ate it. That memory is stuck in my head, the smell and taste of them, the color of them as the sunlight fell on the table. To this day, I can't see, smell, or taste tangerines without thinking about that moment; it's fixed in my memory."

The tangerines meant nothing to me as a psychic, but they meant everything to my client. For her, it was the proof that her mother was with us, because this was not something anyone else would know. And it went way beyond "Your mother is here and she loves you," which is the standard at psychic fairs. A lot of the messages from her mother came after the tangerines, but the tangerines themselves and my perception of that day were what she needed to hear to know her mother was present.

As psychics, we need to learn a new language, the language of symbols. You may remember from chapter 1 that most psychic information comes in through the right brain, the part of our brain that is creative, intuitive, and symbolic. Much of our psychic information comes in the form of symbolism, which is the language of the right side of the brain. While the left side of the brain gets structured, logical, and linear information, the right side of the brain is all about symbols, imagery, and metaphor. Therefore, a critically important skill for psychics to learn is how to interpret these symbol messages. Thankfully, this is a skill that can be learned, and that is what we will cover in this chapter. Whether we are reading the Tarot cards, learning to find psychic messages in our dreams, or catching the meaning of the myriad of signs and omens around us, we need to recognize and then interpret the symbolic meaning of these psychic messages.

In order to do this, we need to shift our attention away from the linear, logical, and literal way that our left brain works. In the left-brain world, a cigar is just a cigar, but the right brain experiences the cigar as metaphor, a symbol for something else. What that might be depends on both our collective and personal associations that we attach to that cigar. Each of us has access to both the collective symbol library and also our personal symbol library. Let's learn a bit more about those now.

The Collective Symbol Library

Carl Jung began the conversation about the *collective symbol library*, which is part of the collective consciousness, the archetypal human psyche that we all share. In his seminal work, *Man and His Symbols*,[3] Jung explains that the human psyche connects with these symbols as a collective and we find similar symbolic meanings throughout humanity. So, whether you are tribal shaman in the Amazon or a housewife from New Jersey, we still connect to these symbols in the same way.

Deb was one of my psychic students and was studying dream interpretation as part of our psychic development classes. Here is a dream she had, followed by the interpretation she came up with after studying the universal symbols in the dream.

✴ DEB'S STORY   *I had a dream where my house was flooded, especially the basement. I was wading through the water, which was filled with things like snakes and rats, and I was very afraid of and disgusted by them. I was determined to get my books though, and once I collected them, I got out of the basement, right before the house caught on fire and fell in on itself. When I studied the universal symbols, I learned that houses represent the psyche, the inner self, so the house was my own being. And the basement represented the subconscious part of the psyche. Water is symbolic of our deep emotions, and lately I have been feeling flooded by these emotions. There were things in the emotional "water" that I was afraid of and grossed out by, like the snakes and rats. I was doing a lot of intense therapy on some of my childhood trauma at the time, and I was looking at some tough emotions. The books represented the knowledge that I was learning about myself, and I was willing to wade through the hard and scary feelings to learn more about myself. And the fire at the end represented total transformation and change. The old me was burning down; it was part of a complete inner transformation and a little trial by fire.*

Deb used the universal, collective symbol library to interpret this dream to her advantage. One can find books on these universal symbols to look up the meanings of dreams, visions, and other symbolic information that we receive as part of our psychic messages. For example, in *A Dictionary of Symbols*[4] by Juan Eduardo Cirlot, you can look up the meanings of the symbols you see in your psychic messages and dreams. Books like this one, and there are many, can be useful tools that can help us learn this collective symbol library, but we also have our own personal symbol library too.

The Personal Symbol Library

Our *personal symbol library* is an amalgamation of our linguistic, familial, societal, and cultural references. It is created from the books we read and movies that we have seen as well as the stories, myths, and fables that were part of our childhood. The challenge of the personal symbol library is figuring out what a particular symbol means to *you*.

One of my psychic friends is a musician, and he receives his psychic downloads as songs that have a lot of meaning and emotion for him. I love movies, and sometimes when my guides are trying to explain a complex situation to me, a scene from a movie will flash into my head, and I know it's relevant to the current situation. The best way to access your personal symbol library is to ask yourself, *What does this mean to me?*

If we go back to Deb's dream, she might have asked herself what the symbols meant to her. In the collective symbol library, books represent knowledge, but does Deb love books or hate them? Maybe she loved them, and they do mean knowledge and books are precious to her. Or maybe they represented a horrible homework chore that she hated. If she loved snakes and rats (some people do, right?), she might have interpreted them as allies who came to help her rather than the scary and gross emotions she was wading through. As a rule, our personal symbol library trumps the collective one, especially if it has a deep meaning to us.

Now remember that we will be interacting with someone else's personal symbol library when we get psychic information for or about them. When this happens, the key is to not interpret it yourself but rather to ask the person what that image means to them.

Let's say that you have a dream that your friend is riding a roller coaster. Maybe you hate roller coasters more than anything, and going on one would be torture for you. If you are using your own symbol library, you might interpret this dream as a bad omen. "Uh oh, I had a dream that you were spinning out of control and you were panicked and it was awful! This is going to be the worst thing that ever happened to you."

But maybe your friend loves roller coasters, and to them it represents the most fun they can possibly have. To keep the interpretation clean, you can ask them, "Hey, I had a dream where you were on a roller coaster. What does that mean to you?" And let them tell you what it means.

Now we know a bit more about how to interpret symbols. Let's move on next to learning how to use these skills to interpret our dreams.

Getting Guidance from Your Dreams

Our dreams are a powerful way to receive guidance. They connect us directly to our subconscious and also to our intuitive and creative side. Dreams can connect us to our own inner guidance, which is our intuition. They also serve as an access point for our guides to communicate with us and as a release valve for our unprocessed emotions, bringing to our attention issues that we have pushed into the shadows of our own subconscious.

Dreams provide such richness to our psychic and spiritual life that it is important to learn how to interpret them. But what if we don't easily remember our dreams? Thankfully, it's easy to train yourself to remember your dreams.

Remembering Your Dreams

Some people have easy access to their dreams. In fact, many visual psychics have a natural ability to remember their dreams. But you don't need to miss out on this gold mine of psychic guidance: you can learn to remember your dreams, even if you don't remember them right now. In general, people dream an average of about two hours a night, and while this happens all through the night, we have more dreams toward the morning hours. Some people swear that they don't dream at all, but actually everyone does. Chances are good that if you feel like you don't dream at all, you just aren't remembering them. However, there are medications and some health conditions like sleep apnea that actually do disrupt our dream cycle.

Tips for Remembering Your Dreams

Here is a recipe that should help you remember your dreams. Try this easy formula; it works with practice and patience.

1. Set a regular sleep schedule and stick to it. Meditation right before bed can considerably increase your ability to remember your dreams.

2. Set your intention to remember your dreams by writing that statement down in your psychic journal: *Tonight, I intend to easily remember my dreams.*

3. Or try drinking a glass of water and declaring, *With this glass of water, I will remember my dreams.* This works well on our subconscious, and if you wake up in the middle of the night to use the bathroom, you may remember what you were dreaming of in the middle of your sleep cycle.

4. Keep your psychic journal next to your bed and write down any little wisp or fragment of your dreams in the morning, even if it's just a feeling. Try not to move around too much, since dreams fade when we wake up fully and shift our brain-wave state into beta. Some people do better with voice recording their dreams than writing them down.

5. We are more apt to remember our dreams if we wake up slowly and naturally. An alarm, especially if you have not had enough sleep, can jolt you into wakefulness so quickly that your dreams fade away

6. Avoid alcohol and drugs before bed since these will interrupt your natural dream cycle.

Dreaming is essential to our well-being and part of our brain's way of processing and integrating all of our experiences. (Scientists now know that animals dream too.) You really can teach yourself to remember your dreams if you practice these techniques with patience and consistency. Right-brained people tend to be more naturally able to remember their dreams; they're also more inclined to be visual psychics. Left-brain dominant people sometimes have to work a little harder to remember their dreams, but it can be done.

Types of Dreams

Now that you are a little more informed about interpreting and remembering your dreams, let's talk about the different types of dreams that we have, and which ones are most relevant to psychic students. There are five different types of dreams that we have through the night, and each of them has a function that is important to our overall health and well-being.

BRAIN SALAD DREAMS

This is not really a technical term, but rather what I call the dreams that we have first thing at night. These dreams often don't have much meaning but are more about the brain clearing itself of unprocessed sensory data. They might be about the TV shows we were watching right before bed, or the book we were reading. They are sometimes about events that happened, especially if we have been too busy to be contemplative. We don't tend to remember them unless we wake up shortly after we have fallen asleep, and we can usually track them to something that happened that day— for example, an unfinished conversation we had with someone or the continuation of the TV show that we had been binge-watching right before bed.

EMOTIONAL DREAMS

Our psyche is always seeking balance and healing and therefore uses emotional dreams as a way to bring unprocessed emotions to our attention. Many of the emotions that we haven't acknowledged and worked through yet with our conscious mind get pushed into our subconscious. I went through a period in my early twenties when I had a recurring dream where I was so angry that I stomped around like Godzilla and smashed buildings in a big city, which I admit to heartily enjoying in my dream. On waking, I was surprised by these dreams since I was one of those people who never let myself get angry. *Hmmm...,* I thought, *I wonder what that was about? I never get angry about anything.* But, in fact, I was not allowing myself to feel angry in my conscious mind, and so pushed all that anger into my subconscious. Once I started dealing with this anger directly, my Godzilla dreams ended.

The most common emotional dream, which I am sure everyone can relate to, is the classic anxiety dream. When we have more anxiety in our lives than we can handle, our psyche will try to balance the equation through an anxiety dream. Here is one of mine: *I am back in high school, even though I am the age that I am now, and I can't remember my locker combination or my class schedule. There is a test in Latin class. I can't find the right classroom and I am late. Did I even take Latin in high school? I wonder who all these people are. Are the mean girls still lurking in the girls' bathroom? Do I have a number two pencil? Oh, yes, and I am in school in my pajamas. Or maybe with no pants on at all. Yikes.*

In anxiety dreams, we are late to the airport, can't find our plane tickets, and we are somehow lost in the wrong city, the wrong country, or even on the wrong planet. These dreams help discharge the emotion of anxiety, and also draw attention to the fact that something is not right with us.

Emotional dreams might bring up any emotion, including sadness, joy, anger, or grief. You know it's an emotion dream because you will feel very emotional in the dream; you might even wake up crying or laughing. We often remember these dreams on waking. It's wise to write them down so you can contemplate them, since doing so can bring about needed emotional healing for you.

RECURRING DREAMS

These are the dreams that repeat over and over again and can be uncomfortable, or they can even be nightmares. They are also your psyche's attempt to find healing and resolution to something that you have not yet fully processed with your entire consciousness. They usually have their roots in unhealed traumas. It's very beneficial to close the loop on these by getting some help with any unresolved traumas, but you can also work on them yourself in your journal by writing a better, more fulfilling ending to the dream. This process works with nightmares too.

PROPHETIC DREAMS

These dreams are very vivid and meaningful. They can be straightforward and easy to understand or steeped in symbolism that we need to decode. Prophetic dreams often foretell someone's passing or pregnancy, or present a clue about something that is coming in the future. There is a psychic message inside a prophetic dream, and our guides will use our dream moments to give us hints, clues, and spiritual bread crumbs to help us find our path. It's an easy way for them to communicate with us directly, since our logical mind is quiet and the symbolic mind is wide open and receptive.

You can identify prophetic dreams by their vividness and by the fact that you're likely to remember them upon waking; they may even stick with you for years afterward. These types of dreams bring a curious neutral emotionality with them, even if it's a topic that you would normally feel very emotional about, like someone's passing.

Here is a great example of a prophetic dream from one of my psychic students: *I recently had to put my dad on hospice care since we knew he was close to death. He kept saying he was happy to go since he wanted to be with my mom again, and she had passed on a few years before that. One night, I had a dream of my mom and dad walking away from me hand in hand down a corridor. I woke up and said to husband that my dad just died, and a few minutes later, I got the phone call that he had died. It was a wonderful gift, and I felt so good knowing my dad was with my mom.*

As I mentioned above, we can identify these dreams by their vividness and their curious lack of emotionality. We also remember them for a long time afterward.

LUCID DREAMS

When we have a *lucid dream*, we are aware that we are dreaming. One part of our consciousness is totally aware that another part of us is dreaming, and we are able to observe our own dreams. Lucid dreaming usually begins as an awareness that we are dreaming, and then becomes an opportunity to change the narrative of our dreams as we dream. Lucid dreams are very powerful, and I have had intense psychic experiences while lucid dreaming. In lucid dreams, we can change the outcome of a nightmare or a recurring dream, such as consciously manifesting a weapon to beat the monster that was chasing you or creating an escape route that wasn't there before. We can even learn to stop the dream by ordering ourselves to wake up or change the narrative of the dream entirely if it gets too intense or disturbing.

If you take the time to record and remember your dreams, you may well be rewarded with lucid dreams. Lucid dreaming is so empowering and healing. As a child, it helped liberate me from a cycle or recurring nightmares where I felt powerless. My very first lucid dream happened when I was still very young and was being chased on a regular basis by some type of monster. I remember thinking that I was just done with feeling powerless and I turned around to face the monster. I grabbed it by its horn and told it that I was no longer afraid of it and that I knew its name. The huge and terrifying monster shrunk to a mouse-sized being and squeaked away, and I never had that dream again. There is such potential power and healing in being able to lucid dream, since it gives us direct access to our subconscious self. I hope you find a way to experience this, if you haven't already.

✳ ✳ ✳

Now that you know about these different types of dreams, I encourage you to record your dreams and see if they are full of psychic information for you. Many visual psychics are strong dreamers and receive their psychic messages this way. One of my students is a medium and gets all her information while she is dreaming. Other people have regular connections with their guides while they are dreaming or have precognitive experiences while dreaming. Dreams can alert us to our own inner emotional needs that require some attention and also clue us into what's going on with the people in our orbit.

Here are some great books about how to get the most out of your dreaming life. I love the work of my friend and mentor Kelly Sullivan Walden, especially *It's All in Your Dreams: Five Portals to an Awakened Life*,[5] which will help you access and remember your dreams. Her wonderful dream dictionary, *I Had the Strangest Dream: A Dream Dictionary for the 21st Century*,[6] is a very useful guide to dream symbolism. Keep them both by your bedside with your psychic journal. Pay attention to your dreams, and dream on!

Signs, Omens, and Synchronicities

As we open up to our psychic abilities, it's very helpful to be able to receive validation of our psychic impressions through signs, omens, and synchronicities. I teach my students to ask for and look for signs after they have received a psychic impression. This can act as a confirmation that a hit was on target, which helps us increase our confidence in own psychic skills.

For example, as you start to communicate with your guides (as we will learn to do in the next chapter), I invite you to ask your guides for proof of their bona fides by offering up a sign that they are for real. It helps us learn to trust that our psychic information is accurate and that we are on the right path as we follow our spiritual bread crumbs along the way.

Signs are literally like signposts that show us our path. They can be anything from pennies that you find that were left for you by your dearly departed, feathers found everywhere, and repeating numbers from your angels, or even magical happenings from the natural world. Signs are direct messages from our guides that we experience in the physical world.

Omens are the harbingers of major changes that are coming our way. Omens can be about major events like impending births and deaths and even larger shifts on the global scale. The word "omen" is defined as being an event that is interpreted as a portent of good or evil. Historically, omens are connected to common superstitions, like seeing a black cat cross your path and breaking a mirror as bad luck.

As modern-day psychic students, however, we are not at the mercy of superstitions, but instead learn to read the energy of the moment. My friend Marcy shared with me an experience that began with what was, for her, a rather chilling omen.

✸ MARCY'S STORY   *I wasn't feeling well for a while and scheduled some doctor visits for diagnostic tests. On my way in to speak with the doctor, three crows landed near my car. They were noisy and squawked and cawed at me, following me through the parking lot. My stomach sank, because for me, seeing three crows is always a bad omen. I felt like they were preparing me to receive bad news from the doctor.*

The omen beforehand helped me prepare myself. By the time that my doctor told me the bad news, I had already started to accept it. But on the way home from that meeting, the sky cleared and a huge, bright double rainbow appeared. It seemed like it was springing right out of my house, so I knew that even though I had a tough diagnosis, I was going to be okay in the end. Something magical would always happen when I was about to lose hope, and it helped me get through a tough time, and I learned a lot about reading the omens around me.

In this example, Marcy referred to her personal symbol library about crows bringing serious news, which supersedes the universal meaning of crows, which is more related to revealing the magic and mystery of the world. But for Marcy, they usually mean something troubling is at hand. She was correct in her interpretation and was given a cancer diagnosis from the doctor. Omens, however, are not always the bearers of bad news, as Marcy discovered with the rainbow over her home. She had a challenging year and spent much of that time looking for more signs and omens, but eventually she was completely healed from the cancer.

Synchronicity, a term coined by Carl Jung, is often explained in the psychological community as the human mind's tendency to make meaning of random patterns and coincidences. But Jung thought that they had a very deep and soulful meaning to them. He defined them as circumstances that appear meaningfully related but lack causal connection. They are experienced as a connected series of events that have meaning to us; they are purposeful signposts that are meant to show us those bread crumbs and confirm that we are on the right path. They are winks from the universe, showing us the path when we feel lost or giving us confirmation that we are headed in the right direction.

One of my psychic students is a young man named Zayne. He was having a moment of doubt about his path and needed to make some decisions. One night he had a dream about the Norse god Odin. Odin had a strong message for him in the dream about which path to take and that he needed courage to take a bold but potentially risky path. Zayne was still unsure about this decision, but the day after the dream, his friend dropped by unexpectedly to show Zayne his new tattoo. It was

Odin's hammer with a message around it in runes. The runes had the same message as Zayne's dream. Just to clear up any lingering doubts that Zayne had, the very next day, another friend brought Zayne some runes as a birthday gift. Zayne asked the runes his question and got the same ones his friend had on his tattoo, the runic version of trust your gut and go for it.

Once we start paying attention to signs, omens, and synchronicities, we will see them everywhere. They can be wonderful confirmation to our psychic impressions.

Here are some common signs, omens, and synchronicities. As we look at these, remember to consider the question "What does this mean to me?" since that can eclipse the more universal meanings.

Repeating Number Sequences. Many people see these on clocks, license plates, store receipts, anywhere where we find numbers in our world. They might be significant, such as birthdays, anniversaries, and death days. Number sequences are a favorite sign from the angels, and there are books, such as *The Angel Numbers Book: How to Understand the Messages Your Spirit Guides Are Sending You*[7] by Mystic Michaela, that give the reader common interpretations for number sequences.

Feathers. Some people find feathers, another favorite of the angels, wherever they go. I had one client who came in for a Reiki session, and as we talked, feathers would appear out of nowhere. She had no down coat with her; they just appeared on the floor and on her clothes and floated through the air. They were almost always white feathers. She connected the appearance of these feathers as confirmation from the angels that she was walking the right path.

Interpreting Repeating Number Sequences

Let's take a look at some interpretations of the most common repeating number sequences, just to give you a quick guide. These are sourced from many different places and come more from a collective, universal symbol library that includes angel numbers, numerology, and sacred geometry and mathematics. These numbers can be single, double, or triple numbers, or they can even come in sequences of four numbers such as 11-11. Don't forget that your personal meanings for these take precedence over the universal meanings, so asking yourself what these numbers mean to you can be very productive and illuminating.

✳ **1s and 11-11:** This is the number of beginnings and the gateway to new things, which represents the threshold. You are on the verge of something new, and it's up to you to walk through the gateway. Many people see these numbers on digital clocks.

✳ **2s:** You are at a moment of choice. Look for the balance point. There are two paths in front of you. Look into your heart and ask for guidance to help you choose. This number might also mean you have made the right choice.

✳ **3s:** Three is the number of the ascended masters and the highest levels of consciousness that humanity can achieve. It's the number of Christ and represents his ascension to the higher planes of consciousness.

✳ **4s and especially 444:** This is the number of the angels and is a sign that angels are around you offering guidance and support.

✳ **5s:** Change is upon you. Things are breaking up and deconstructing so that your life can form in a newer and higher way. It might be uncomfortable as things shift, but it's good to have faith that, in the long run, the change will be beneficial for you.

✳ **6s:** You may have overreached yourself and are now out of balance. Sometimes 6 also represents stagnation and the need for change. Refocus your energy and take full responsibility for yourself and your life. Grounding practices can be helpful here.

✳ **7s:** Seven is the number of magic and manifestation. Keep your thoughts and desires on what you want to create in your life, and you will have divine assistance in creating what you desire.

✳ **8s:** Eight is the number of abundance. The message is to harvest what you have sown and be grateful for the bounty in your life. This is the number of infinite possibility, and it also invites us to reap the rewards of our hard work and reminds us that deep gratitude can bring us more abundance.

✳ **9s:** Nine is a completion number that symbolizes the end of a cycle. Take a moment to honor the ending of things as part of the normal cycle of life: something ends so something new can begin.

✦ **0:** This is the null point, the empty space into which something new comes into being. If we see it, we are being called to wait, like a fallow field, for something new to be planted there.

Other number sequences usually relate to birthdays, anniversaries, and death days.

Coins. Long connected to messages from our dearly departed, these "pennies from heaven" validate that our loved ones are present. One of my psychic students shared a story about how her grandmother used to slip her lunch money into her mitten so she wouldn't lose the coins on the way to school. After her grandmother passed, she would find quarters in her gloves and knew that her grandmother was still looking out for her.

Music. We can receive messages from and have contact with our loved ones through music. Listen to what songs show up on the radio, and pay attention to the songs as you walk into stores too. If this is one of your signs, try asking your guides a question and then putting your playlist on random to see if a message comes through.

Augury. This is defined as finding signs and omens in the appearance and behavior of animals and the natural world, especially the weather. I have a strong connection to animals and often receive messages from them. I watch for unusual behavior from the wild animals around me and know that certain animals bring strong messages with them. Just yesterday, I was pondering a change in my life, and I came to a crossroads near my house. There was a doe with a fawn standing in the middle of a fairly busy intersection. The doe stared at me for a long while and then took the rockier, dirt road path out of the intersection. I knew it was a message for me to take the more challenging, less traveled path too. Animals may show up in real life, but they can also appear in our dreams, on TV, and as images everywhere we go.

Weather. Many find their signs and omens in the elements and the patterns of the weather, which is also considered a part of augury. One my teachers is a shaman, and she had a strong connection to the element of air. The wind would gust or pick up when something was coming her way, and she always knew if it was an "ill wind" or a beneficial one, like the winds of change. Paying attention to wind, rain, and lightning and being able to read the messages in fire and water are part of this. Staring into fire, water, smoke, and crystals is an old and honored way to find messages; that is where the idea of a psychic gazing into a crystal ball came from.

✳ ✳ ✳

So, how do you tell the difference between a real sign, omen, or synchronicity and just a plain old coincidence? These types of signs happen in a slightly extraordinary way, and they feel significant and out of the ordinary. You can have a yard full of squirrels and it's not a sign—it's just life happening around you. However, if you go outside and the squirrel drops an acorn on your head, or is waiting for you on the roof of your car and giving you the squint eye, it's more likely to be a sign.

Signs, omens, and synchronicities have a feeling of the nonordinary. If you are paying attention, they feel significant, even weighty, and there is something unusual about them. Signs feel magical and happen in an extraordinary way. Once I was driving fairly quickly down a winding back road, and suddenly a red cardinal flew into my car through the open passenger side window and then back out the driver's side window. To put the exclamation point on it all, it dropped a red feather in my lap on the way through. I had just asked for a sign, and I got a memorable one! My life has always abounded in signs, omens, and synchronicities, and I depend on them to move myself forward.

You have now mastered the art of watching for and interpreting signs, omens, and synchronicities. Next, let's look at how we can create more opportunities for them to come along by learning to use some divination tools.

Using Divination Tools

Does the word "divination" conjure up images of a fortune-teller in a lacy shawl, gazing into a crystal ball, pulling Tarot cards, and telling you that you will meet a tall, dark stranger before the new year begins? Or perhaps you only know it as Harry Potter's least favorite class at Hogwarts. The image is a cliché, but it has its roots in something real. Psychics have long used divination tools to help them connect with psychic information, and clichés aside, it's a very helpful practice.

Divination is defined as the art of being able to tell the future, and yet as psychic students, we can use it for gathering all kinds of psychic information and not just about the future. *Divination tools* are objects and systems that help us focus our energy and also act as a gateway, a midway point, between ourselves and our guides. Your guides will use your divination practice as a method to communicate directly with you. Using your divination tools daily will also help you exercise your psychic muscles and give you a chance to practice interpreting symbols.

I could say that divination tools are like training wheels, a way to help us move along the path until we have strengthened our psychic muscles so much that we no longer need to use the tools to make our psychic connection. However, that would be doing them and the process of using them a disservice, since honestly, I still use them myself all the time.

When I was a beginner psychic and just starting out doing readings for other people, I used them as kind of a safety measure. I would have my clients pull the Tarot cards, and the ritual of it helped me make my psychic connection. I never worried about coming up dry, because I always had the cards to fall back on, and being that relaxed and confident about it also helped keep me in the alpha brain-wave state so that I was able to tune in when I needed to.

I still have a daily practice of using the cards and a few other divination tools for my own life decisions and to help me read the energy of the day. We tend to lose our psychic connection when we get emotionally triggered about things, which makes it very difficult to read for yourself when you are upset or anxious about something. Because of that, being able to check in with your divination tools is really handy.

Choosing a Divination Tool

Now that we know why we use them, let's look at how we pick one. There are many different kinds of divination tools, and they are all good. Choosing one is generally a matter of preference and resonance. It's a great time to tap into your intuition and see if you feel called to one type or another. You might experience this as having a curiosity or interest about one of them, or perhaps you might keep seeing or hearing about one of them. I felt like mine was chosen for me, when one of my friends gave me a deck of the Rider-Waite Tarot cards when I was about sixteen years old. It's not the easiest oracle deck to master, but I always felt a connection to it and have spent much time since then using, studying, and teaching people how to use this classic Tarot deck.

If you have a spiritual bookshop near you, wander around and see which decks of cards or other tools you might be drawn to using. Shops like this will sometimes let you take the cards out and look at them. I recommend trying several on for size and then narrowing it down to a few so you can gain some confidence, comfortability, and skill in using them.

Here are some common divination tools. There are, of course, many more available than are listed here.

TAROT CARDS

The Tarot (which rhymes with "sparrow" and not "carrot") is a complex and rich system of teaching that is chock-full of old mystery school wisdom. The classic Rider-Waite deck is a wonderful deck to learn on, and the images on the cards are rich with symbolism. I recommend starting with this classic deck, since the deeper meaning is often lost in the more modern interpretation of the Tarot.

It's essential to have a good reference book for these cards, and it does take time to learn them. Or better yet, take a class and study with a teacher until you understand the system. Add a simple three-card spread to your daily practice and record the results in your psychic journal. Or you can learn more complex card spreads, such as the classic Celtic cross, for insight into complex issues.

In defense of the Tarot deck, there is no association to black magic, nor are they anything to be scared of. People have made this assumption due to the Devil and Death cards in the deck, which have everything to do with steps along the spiritual path, and are not about dark magic at all.

ORACLE CARDS

There are many of these decks, and they are much easier to use right out of the box than the traditional Tarot cards. They do come with little books in the decks to help you find deeper meaning, but most have the meaning of the card written right on it. You can find general oracle decks or ones that focus on issues like relationships and life purpose. There are too many to mention specific ones here, but I love the decks of Collette Baron-Reid, which are both beautiful and wise.

Go with your intuition and try a few out; they are rich with meaning and easy to use. One can find decks based on goddesses, the ascended masters, mermaids and fairies, mythical and divine beings from every pantheon you can think of. Many are whimsical and charming, and most have good wisdom too.

ANGEL CARDS

If you feel a special connection to angels, then getting a deck of angel cards can help you learn to communicate with them directly. Angels are so high frequency that many psychic students benefit from having a special card deck that helps them connect to these divine beings. We will talk more about how to connect with them directly in chapter 11.

RUNES

Arising from the old Norse alphabet, runes are used now as a divination tool. The twenty-four runic letters are most often carved onto stones or wooden disks that come inside their own little bag, although you can also get them as a card deck. To read them, put them in their bag and shake up the bag. Ask your question and then pull out a rune. Looking up the meanings of the runes in the book that accompanies them will give you some insight and answers.

I CHING

This is an ancient and complex divination system from China and is thought to be the oldest divination system still in use, dating back over three thousand years. The I Ching, also known as "The Book of Changes," uses a number system to create the hexagrams, which are a guide to living according to the philosophies of Confucianism, Taoism, and Buddhism. Modern I Ching systems use coins and a reference book, although the old school way to do it was to toss yarrow sticks and look for the pattern.

You consider your question and then throw the three coins, or toss your yarrow sticks, to create the hexagram. This is a complex system that requires study and some reference books too. Try *The I Ching or Book of Changes: A Guide to Life's Turning Points: The Essential Wisdom Library*[8] by Brian Browne Walker as a good starting point.

DOWSING

Dowsing is an ancient and fascinating system of divination; dowers use dowsing rods to help them pinpoint locations for things like water or to find lost articles. The rods can be made from anything, but copper is the most common. Some are single rods that are Y-shaped and others are a pair of two L-shaped rods with the dowser holding the short parts of the Ls in their hands. Traditional dowsers use their tools to find water and are highly accurate.

Just the other day, my friend used his pendulum to dowse for the underground roots of trees so we could avoid them while planting. Dowsers can use their tools to get yes/no/I-don't-know answers to questions. Dowsing is fantastic for finding things like wells, underground water, and for reading energy, such as the lay lines of the earth, which are the energy meridians of the earth itself. It has limitations as a divination tool due to the difficult nature of boiling down complex human behavior into a yes/no binary as we discussed in chapter 1.

✳ ✳ ✳

Now that you have learned a little bit about divination tools, I recommend that you go out and acquire some. These tools will add richness to your psychic messages and give you a chance to practice your symbol interpretation, exercise your psychic muscle, and give your guides a direct method to communicate with you. Once you get a divination tool, it's important to learn how to cleanse your tool of any random energy that it has collected before it got to you.

> ### PSYCHIC TIP: *Cleansing Your Divination Tools*
>
> No matter which divination tool you use, it's essential to cleanse the tool before you use it. If you buy a new deck of oracle cards, for example, open the deck and use sage spray or smoke to clear the deck of residual energy. You can also rest it on top of a bowl of salt. You can charge the deck by letting it sit out in the sun or the moonlight. I recommend carrying it in your purse or pocket for a while to let the deck attune to your energy. It's polite to always ask permission before you touch someone else's divination tool and also good to clear and recharge it after you use it.

Using Your Tools for Readings

Now that you have a divination tool or two at the ready, the best way to master them and also increase your intuition in the process is to use them on a regular basis. Make some time every day to check in with your intuition and open up your psychic sense by using the tools. Let's say, for example, that you have an oracle deck. Try to find ten to fifteen minutes a day to practice with it. Adding this time to your meditation routine can be a great opportunity to practice.

Try pulling a card every day and then recording it in your psychic journal. I use a few different decks and pull cards from each one every day. My current favorites are the Rider-Waite Tarot deck, an animal card deck, and a goddess card deck. I shuffle each one and pull a card from each deck. I consider them and will often see a pattern or theme across the decks. I record them in my journal and then the following day, before I pull new ones, I contemplate them again and ask myself, *How was my day like that? What did I think was going to happen and what really did happen? Did the cards reflect the day that I actually had?* And then I pull new ones for the current day.

There are many other ways to use them too. You can pull a daily three-card spread like one of these:

- What is the energy of the past, the present, the future? What is the energy of yesterday, today, and tomorrow?

- What is going on today in body, mind, and spirit?

- Where am I now, where am I going, and what do I need to do to get there?

- For a relationship, try pulling one card for yourself, one for the other person, and one for the relationship between you.

There is a huge benefit in learning at least one divination tool and adding it to your daily psychic practice. It will help exercise your psychic muscle and also provide a direct connection between you and your guides.

Now that you have learned to pay attention to and interpret your dreams plus all the signs, omens, and synchronicities that are around you, I know that you will begin to have richer and more plentiful psychic experiences. It's worth putting the effort into learning this new language, since it is the lexicon of psychic experiences.

What's Next?

In our next chapter, we will take the skills that we have learned in the last three chapters so that we can use them to speak directly to our guides. We will explore this whole concept of guides and who they really are. We'll examine some common misconceptions about how our guides interact with us as well as how we can deeply benefit from working with them.

Let's dig in.

Chapter 5

Work with Your Guides

Now that we have covered the foundational skills that all psychic students need, we are ready to dive into the concept of guides. *Guide* is an umbrella term that I use to describe the beneficial, nonphysical beings that are around us. Their purpose is to help us in our spiritual and personal evolution. It's a pretty hard place to incarnate, here on planet Earth. It's difficult physically and emotionally, and as our souls choose to come here to learn, mature, and evolve, we face many challenges. Our guides offer us assistance, support, and guidance, since as incarnated humans we are on the front lines and we need all the help we can get.

I have experienced my own guides my whole life, so it doesn't seem like a strange concept to me. In fact, my very first memory is of lying in my crib and being surrounded by a group of luminous beings. They were waving, smiling, cooing, and blowing me kisses, and I felt so much love for them and from them. Then my mother came in through the door and walked right through them, clearly without seeing them. This is not only my first memory of guides, but it's my first memory ever!

In all the readings that I have done over the years, I have never met anyone that didn't have a whole team of guides with them. Even people who would never consider the possibility that they have spiritual help here still have guides with them. You don't have to know about them in order to have them still assist you.

A psychic that I knew long ago told me that he believed that our world was populated with equal amounts of living humans, benevolent spirit guides, and less helpful disincarnate entities and that this is a unique situation in the cosmos. This rings true to me, and although I am not sure why there is such a preponderance of spiritual beings here, it does correlate with my experience.

Many different types of beings can be on our spirit guide team, and who is with us can change over time, depending on where we are in our life's journey. Some guides stay with us our whole life and even appear in many, or all, of our lifetimes; others come and go as we need them. Some are personal and work only with us, like your Uncle Julio, while others work with whoever calls them in, like Mother Mary.

Assuming our guides are actually real and are very powerful beings, it's easy to wonder why they don't just handle all our problems for us. There are certain parameters involved here that include rules and agreements that are important to understand about this type of relationship.

How Our Guides Operate in Our Lives

There are rules about how our guides can operate in our lives. For the most part, they can't violate our free will. Free will is one of the most important laws of this dimension. Our choices have a lot of power, and guides can't overwrite the choices we make; they can't save us from the results of our choices either. They may whisper into our ear "Are you sure you really want to do that?" but they can't stop us if we are about to make a bad decision.

Except when they do.

There are some times when your guides will show up and literally save your life. You might have heard stories about mysterious strangers who materialize from nowhere and pull someone out of the burning wreckage of their car and then are never seen again. These things do sometimes happen, but it is a mystery to me why sometimes they save you and sometimes they don't. I wonder if we all have a few "get out of jail free" cards that we can use in these cases.

I remember jumping off the roof of my parents' garage when I was a kid, since I was absolutely certain that I could actually fly. Of course, gravity predictably kicked in and I fell. I swear that I felt an angelic hand grab me by my ankle, slow my fall, and move me about three feet from the hard driveway to the nice squishy compost pile. I was bruised and got the wind knocked out of me but was relatively undamaged, considering. I did get an angelic scolding along the lines of *What were you thinking? Do you know hard it was to get you on this planet at this time? About a thousand miracles had to happen to get you here now, in this body, in this time frame, and you can't be dying now because you have really important things to do when you grow up...*

We do sometimes get that miracle, and sometimes we don't. Maybe it's because we've used up our miracles already. Or maybe it's because it was our appointed time to go. Or perhaps we do need to learn to deal with the results of our choices even if that means game over. However, it is best to take full responsibility for your choices, your thoughts, words, and deeds since that is how we grow and mature spiritually.

Our guides can't and won't take away our lessons for us. We all have things to learn here, and mostly we do that by making choices and then experiencing the consequences of our own actions. When we are rescued from having to deal with these consequences, we lose the opportunity to learn from them and can end up making the same mistakes over and over again. If you are a parent, you wouldn't do your kids' homework for them, right? If you did, they wouldn't really learn anything, might fail their test, or end up not knowing something that they should know later in life when they really need it. In just the same way, our guides will offer compassion, support, hints, and clues to an easier path, but they won't take away the hard work of living from us.

The same is true for the free will of other people. It's no use asking your guides to "make" someone do something you want them to. Overriding other people's free will is a form of black magic, and therefore it is something your guides certainly won't do—and neither should you. I am not saying you shouldn't pray or send good juju to someone, but just try and check your agenda at the door. Your guides will have limited ability to protect other people, but the exception to this is with children. You can send your angels off with your children for general protection, and they will do what they can.

And, of course, we use common sense, right? Please do pray and ask your angels to protect you while you are on a road trip, but do your part by wearing your seat belt and driving sensibly.

Some of us—these tend to be people who don't like being told what to do—have guides that work with us in a very hands-off way. If you are a person who likes to do things yourself and figure things out on your own, then your guides will have a lighter touch with you. They might make suggestions, or they may not offer any suggestions at all until you ask them directly for help. Other people have more hands-on, directive guides. Mine are like that, and I joke around and say that I just show up and do what I am told. I have had this arrangement with my guides since I can remember.

Even if you have bossy guides like I do, a true guide is a benevolent being who will not criticize or belittle you. They will make suggestions, but they are never mean, nor would they tell you to do something that was not in your highest good.

You can increase your connection with your guides if you ask for help on a daily basis. This helps them connect with us, since we are engaging our free will by asking for help. There are days when I ask for help before my feet even hit the floor in the morning: *Hey Team, I am not sure what I need today, but please just help me!* Or we might ask more directly for things like courage, healing, compassion, or clarity from our guides.

The Rules That Guides Follow

Here are some good rules of thumb to keep in mind about working with your guides.

- ✸ It's a relationship that needs to be nurtured, and the more time you spend trying to communicate with them, the more they will show up.

- ✸ They can't detour around your free will or take away the consequences of your own actions and choices.

- ✸ They are here to empower you, not take away your power. Don't fall into the trap of asking them to make your decisions for you or shuffling off your personal responsibilities onto them.

- ✸ They won't interfere with the free will of others either, so although sometimes we can ask our guides to help out others, they can't and won't go against someone else's free will.

- ✸ Real guides are never mean or critical, nor would they tell you to do something harmful to yourself or anyone else.

Now you understand the basic rules of engagement that we have with our guides. Next, let's explore the many ways that we can connect with our guides, receive their messages, and create a stronger relationship with them.

Connecting with Your Guides

As you go through the exercises in this book, you will be connecting with more than one guide. It's a good idea to record any information that you receive about your guides in your psychic journal so you can keep track of your experiences and what you are learning about your team along the way.

It's important to know that, when we meet our guides for the first time, we need to relax, to have fun with it, and to drop expectations of what we might experience. Our logical mind can get in the way when we make decisions ahead of time—like "This is going to be hard, I won't be able to do it" or "My guide is going to be a unicorn because I love unicorns." If you can, it's best to be a blank slate and tune in to what you actually experience in the moment, since people will sometimes ignore or push away what is there if it doesn't meet their expectations.

By now you already have an idea about which are your strongest psychic senses. If you know your primary psychic sense is clairaudience, then really listen in, since your guides will use the channels that are already the most open for you.

If you are anxious or fearful about the process, chances are good that your guides will choose to come in very softly so they don't scare you. If they freak you out too much, then they risk having you give up in a fright. If that happens, you'll never take the chance to connect with them again, so they will err on the side of being too quiet rather than to risk frightening you. I want to share what happened to my psychic student Rashad as he first consciously connected to his guides. He was working through the fears that both he and his family had about his psychic experiences. Rashad had been experiencing spirits his entire life, and his Muslim faith proclaims that speaking to spirits is not a good idea.

✴ RASHAD'S STORY   *The first time that I tried the Meet Your Guide Meditation, I was so nervous that some devil was going to pop up and scare me, that all I saw was a little pink glow in my field of vision and a faint feeling of happiness. I felt warmth in my heart and a quiet sense that I was safe, and it was all going to be okay. I really did feel safe, and as I practiced over time, the pink glow got clearer and clearer, and eventually I could see a figure of a beautiful woman standing there. She was so wise and peaceful and has helped me tremendously since then. Now I wonder how I could ever have been afraid of her.*

Our relationship with our guides is just that—a relationship. We must put our time into the process to develop that relationship. The best way to do this is to make connecting with your guides part of your daily routine. This can be your daily card pulls, so ask your guides to connect with you through your cards. If you have a routine of daily meditation, you might ask your guides if they have something to say to you as part of your meditation practice. There are also many wonderful guided meditations that will give you an opportunity to commune with your guides. And don't forget to pay attention to all your psychic senses, since our guides will connect with us through all of them. Those hunches, nudges, and knowings are very likely direct messages to you from your guides.

How to Connect with Your Guides

Here are some guidelines and best practices about how to connect with your spirit guides.

- ❀ They may come to you very quietly at first, since the last thing they want to do is scare you. If you are nervous about this, expect them to come in gently.

- ❀ Try to drop any expectations about what you think *should* be happening and be present with what *is* actually happening.

- ❀ Expand your awareness to all your psychic senses: you may sense, know, hear, feel, taste, smell, or see something. You might feel a presence, sense a color, or hear a ringing in your ears.

- ❀ This is a relationship that is created over time, so be patient and try often to connect.

- ❀ Ask for a sign, omen, or synchronicity from your guides to help you know it's really them.

- ❀ Use your pendulum to confirm the information you get or break out the divination tools to give your guides an easy way to communicate.

It's very helpful to build trust with your guides by asking them to send you some kind of sign, omen, or synchronicity that they are the real deal. This is part of building trust and faith in your guides. Just like you wouldn't really listen to a complete stranger without checking out their bona fides, the same will hold true with your guides. Ask for something specific, like a penny or a feather, and see what shows up in the next day or two. It takes time and connection to build trust with a guide, so don't rush this.

I know that if you take up these practices, you will build a beautiful relationship with your guides over time. Now let's take a look at all the different roles that they can play with us.

Our Guides' Roles with Us

Our guides work and interact with us through a variety of functions and roles. When I meet a guide for the first time, I always ask what their function is, since it really helps to know this. Some guides have a very singular purpose, while other ones can fulfill many different functions all at once. Let's look at a few of the roles that they fill for us.

Teachers

These guides are around to help you learn a particular subject. If you are a college student or you are studying a healing method or a spiritual teaching, you might attract a guide whose job it is to help you learn that subject. My friend Sue, who is a wonderful healer and shaman, shared this experience.

✸ SUE'S STORY   *I was doing my first healing on a friend, and I looked beside me and I saw a Native American man standing next to me. He had long black hair and a cigarette hanging out of the corner of his mouth. He was wearing jeans and a white T-shirt with a black leather vest. I was so surprised to see him standing beside me. He directed me in that healing since I really didn't know what I was doing, and he has been with me when I do healings ever since, especially when I am learning something new.*

Event- or Project-Specific Guides

These beings show up for a certain event or a time in your life—for example, while you are working at a particular job, going through a significant life event, or traveling somewhere. You may have one while you are writing your dissertation or completing a big project at work. I had a guide who was just around me while I was pregnant; it was this guide's specialty. These guides tend to be around for a certain time period and then they move on.

Muses

People who are very creative will often feel they are channeling the music they are playing, the art they are creating, or the words they are writing. They feel guided from an outside source. This type of guide is called a *muse*, and their purpose is to inspire us in the creative process.

Many people undervalue creativity as a spiritual pursuit, but my friend and colleague Jacob Nordby says in his book *The Creative Cure: How Finding and Freeing Your Inner Artist Can Heal Your Life*[9] that creativity is a direct and pure expression of our soul, and therefore the muses should be honored as very important guides.

If you have these types of guides around you, you will notice that you get swept up in the creative process as if the words, music, or art is flowing through you. There is a very significant connection between the intuitive and creative side of us as they really spring up out of the same part of our brain and our being. Check out the lovely book *The Way of the Empath: How Compassion, Empathy, and Intuition Can Heal Your World*[10] by artist and healer Elaine Clayton for more tips on how to use creativity to open up and explore your intuition.

Healers

These guides work with us to help us heal from whatever is troubling us. They can help us in mind, body, or spirit, whatever we need in the moment. They often come to us when we are sleeping and do the work of healing then. They can help us heal at all levels of our being, whether it is emotional, mental, physical, or spiritual. I asked some of the guides that work with me why they so often help heal us while we sleep, and they said that we naturally go into a healing and restorative cycle while we sleep and that the resistance to the work is lower when our conscious minds are out of the picture.

Antonio is one of my Reiki students. He learned Reiki to help him recover from a serious, chronic illness that he had been struggling with since he was a child.

✳ ANTONIO'S STORY   *I was sick for a long time, and a couple of years ago, everything got much worse and I wasn't sure that I was going to make it. I did a lot of Reiki on myself, and worked with a team of doctors and healers. Every night, I would pray before I went to sleep and ask my healing guides to help me heal.*

One night, I had a dream that I was in a room full of luminous beings—it almost felt like a surgical suite full of glowing people. They asked me if I really wanted to stay in my body or if I was ready to leave and go back home to spirit world.

They told me that if I stayed, it was going to be hard and that I needed to do some deeper emotional healing. Or, if I was tired, I could just let go. I knew that

I was at a very significant choice point, and I know that if I had decided to leave, I would have probably died in my sleep that night—I was that sick. But I chose to stay and do the work. Every night after that, I could sense the beings working with me to heal, and I did. I had a remission that will probably make the medical textbooks since there is no known cure for the disease that I used to have. I am still working on regaining my full health, but I am so grateful for my healing guides and I am still happy to be here.

Healer guides are wonderful beings to work with. They offer comfort, companionship, and unconditional love, which we all need!

Spiritual Directors

These might be the most important guides that we have. Their function is to help guide and direct us on our spiritual path, and they are often connected to us through many lifetimes. They get the big picture of our whole evolution as a being, they know the karmas that we are working through, and they can access our karmic record by seeing our past life history. And they understand our life purpose, and keep track of our soul contracts with other people too. They will help show us the way by giving us hints, hunches, and nudges to help us find our path, and they open the right doors for us with synchronicities. They will also be with us when we pass away and move into the next realm; their purpose then is to help us review our life, understand all the lessons learned and wisdom gained in that incarnation, and also help us choose our next one based on what we most need to experience.

We can connect with spiritual directors easily in our dreams, and it's very common for them to visit with us while we sleep and to give us advice and course corrections that then later filter down into our conscious minds. Even people who have no conscious idea that they are psychic or have guides will connect with their spiritual director while they sleep.

They have a lot of compassion, but they are not usually a hand-holding type of guide. Their purpose is rather to push us out of our comfort zone so that we can grow in all ways. Sometimes when we resist this growth, they will help create a circumstance that will lever us out of a dysfunctional job or relationship that we don't quite have the courage to leave on our own.

My psychic student Cindy has a spiritual director that looks like a mountaineer. He has ropes, climbing equipment, and a backpack full of helpful items for her. And he carries a lamp that he shines at her feet so she can see her path. Another one of my students has a trio of ancient-looking sages who offer wisdom and philosophies about the meaning of life. They point out the many choices that he has in front of him but are not directive at all; they consider all choices valid and part of the "research" of living. They are serious, gentle hearted, and compassionate, just like my student is.

In total contrast to this, when I recently did a session for one of my clients, I saw two old ladies who were laughing, slapping each other on the back, and telling dirty jokes. They were her spiritual directors, and they were earthy, irreverent, and a little bossy. Their message to my client was to lighten up. Since she took everything so seriously, she needed to relax and go with the flow a little more. This was their message to her: *Your path is in the flow of joy, love, pleasure, and fun. You need to live fully in each moment and learn to be peaceful with not knowing what is going to happen next. Loosen your grip and keep choosing love.*

Protectors and Guardians

These guides are like bodyguards, and they offer us their protection in many different ways. Their protection can extend to all areas of our lives, including physical, emotional, mental, psychic, and energetic. This can be very useful, especially for very sensitive empaths.

Our protector guides help us remain safe by avoiding dicey situations. They might whisper into your ear to help you avoid real danger as they did with my friend Wendy.

✴ WENDY'S STORY   *In my early twenties, I was in a big state forest taking photographs. I was alone by a riverbank, and I heard a very loud voice inside my head say,* Go!!! Get in your car right now! *It felt as if I was also pushed when I heard it. As I got to my car, a man drove by very slowly, and I got the chills and felt very cold. It felt like a shark circling around the parking lot, and I was glad to be safe in my car, driving away. I know that I avoided contact with a predator that day, and I still get chills when I think about it.*

We all have protector spirits with us. It is very good to make a conscious connection with them so that we can continue to be safe in the world.

> ## PSYCHIC TIP: *Calling in Your Protectors*
>
> We can call on our guardians when we don't feel safe or need energetic protection. Take a few centering and grounding breaths and then ask for protection: "Guardians and protectors, send help now!" You can ask for something specific, or you can send out a more general SOS. Once you have done this, look for the signs, omens, and synchronicities to show you the way.

Gatekeepers

These beings work mostly with mediums, and their function is to make connections for us across the spiritual realms. They hold open the "gates" and doors between worlds so we can access different dimensions. All mediums have these guides that guard the doorways between the world of the living and the dead. If you feel like you have mediumship abilities, the gatekeepers are essential to know about. They are important because they will keep unwanted spirits out and also help usher in any spirits of the departed that you want to communicate with.

If not done properly, mediumship can be a little dangerous. Inexperienced mediums open the door to the astral plane (which we will discuss at length in chapter 6), which is where ghosts and other uneasy spirits reside. This is why séances in the hands of novices are not recommended. They open doors to the other side, and if you don't know how to properly close those doors, astral beings can follow you home. Our gatekeeper guides help us close these doors and manage the flow between realms.

Gatekeeper guides come in many different varieties. My colleague Deb works with her grandmother, who was also a medium and an old-school Portuguese healer. Her nonna keeps unhelpful spirits away when Deb is working and ushers in the ones she really wants to speak with.

✻ DEB'S STORY *It's pretty common when I am doing sessions that many dead people show up. Maybe only a few of them are relevant to the session that I am doing, but the room gets very crowded with curious spirits or the stuck ones who just want to butt in on the session. Nonna keeps them in order. She was a powerhouse in life, and she is still that way for me now!*

Sasha is a powerful medium who connects with the Celtic goddess Cerridwen as her gatekeeper. Long an associate of the Greek goddess Hecate, Cerridwen guards the gates between worlds and stands at the crossroads between life and death. Sasha told me that since she started asking this guide to open and then close the gateways before and after her sessions, her office is very quiet and peaceful. "Before I knew how to do that," Sasha said, "it felt like there was a line of spirits outside, waiting to crowd in and all wanting to talk at once. Now only the relevant ones are there, and I am not bothered by random wayward spirits in the middle of the night."

These are fascinating examples of the roles that our guides play for us. And there are also many types of guides. This goes beyond their function to what type of being they are. For example, you might have a protector guide that is a power animal, a departed relative, or nature spirit. For more on these different types of guides, see the text box "Guides That Commonly Associate with Us."

Guides That Commonly Associate with Us

As far as I can tell, there is an infinite variety of spirit guides. Through all the years that I have been working as a psychic and communicating with other people's guides, I have continued to discover new types of guides, some that I have never seen before. And yet, for the most part, I encounter the same types of guides that very commonly associate with and assist humanity. We will go deeply into each type of guide later in the book, but here is a little thumbnail view of the ones that associate the most with humanity.

- ⊛ **Ancestor Spirits:** These guides are the souls of our loved ones who have crossed over and help us from the other side. They can be great advisers, protectors, and cheerleaders that are here to help boost our energy and morale.

- ⊛ **Angels:** Beloved by people, angels are intermediaries between God and humanity. They are not human spirits, so we don't die and become an angel. They are divine messengers, and their function is to assist us in our elevation back to divine consciousness.

- ⊛ **Ascended Masters, Prophets, and Saints:** These are souls that used to be human but have evolved beyond the cycle of reincarnation. They are enlightened beings who continue to teach, inspire, and heal humanity, but from the position of a spirit guide rather than an incarnated person. They are available to anyone who asks for their help. They include people like Jesus, Mary, the Buddha, Krishna, and Kuan-yin.

⊛ **Beings of Pure Energy:** There is a seemingly infinite variety of these beings that are hard to classify. They are high-level spiritual beings that aren't human, and they exist mostly of energy. They often show up in the role of spiritual director, teacher, or healer guides.

⊛ **Earth Spirits:** These are the denizens of the fairy realms and are the spiritual essences of the natural world, including plant spirits and spirit essences of the elements. They are the spirits of rocks, trees, mountains, rivers, lakes, forests, and individual plants.

⊛ **Multidimensional Beings:** These beings are from many different places and serve many different purposes, but the main characteristic of these is that they aren't from around here but come from some other dimension.

⊛ **Power Animals:** These are the energy and essential wisdom of the spirit of animals. Their pure, simple energy assists us by bringing in particular frequencies—for example, the lion brings us courage, strength, and leadership qualities when we need that energy.

⊛ **Soul Family Guides:** These guides are part of our "soul family" rather than our biological family. These are your soul mates who are not incarnated with you at present, but who still bring their love, presence, and wisdom to you.

What do we do when we encounter a spirit that doesn't feel good to us? They are around, but as long as we have our wits about us and are practicing discernment, we can handle this. Here is how.

Guides vs. Entities: Basic Discernment Skills

We have already discussed that not all beings we might contact are helpful spirits. There are nonhelpful spirits that we might encounter as we practice meeting guides.

Psychic students often worry about how to tell the difference between a real guide, which always has your best intentions at heart, and an entity that doesn't.

Discernment is the ability to tell what kinds of spirits we are dealing with. Just to reassure you, you already do this without effort, probably ten times a day. Let's take the example of what happens when you meet a person for the first time. Your intuitive self makes a snap judgment within a few minutes or sometimes even seconds of an introduction, and you already know if that person resonates with you or not.

Spiritual and psychic discernment isn't any different. Whether it involves living people, dead people, or any other type of spirit, the process of discernment is the same.

You will feel, sense, or know right off the bat if someone or something is

- good, benevolent, and helpful,

- neutral, or

- bad, mischievous, or malevolent

Check in to see how your body feels. If a person or a spirit sends out negative energy, even if it looks good on the surface, you will feel bad. Are you getting cold, clammy, or nauseated? Maybe your belly is tight and your breathing is constricted. Do you feel funky and uneasy? Tune in to what your gut knowing is telling you. Check in with how you feel and what you know. Expand this to all your psychic senses, and you may also see and hear things that will help you make an evaluation.

The same will be true if you encounter either a helpful person or a true spirit guide. You are going to feel good. Maybe you feel warm, uplifted, and safe. Perhaps you relax, and your belly and breathing softens. You feel, know, sense, or perceive that this is a beneficial being.

Or perhaps you feel neither bad nor good, but rather something neutral. Neutral spirits are very common, and psychic students encounter them because as you open up, you light up the astral plane like a little lightbulb. The neutral spirits are curious, and they come around to check you out, a little bit like moths to a candle flame. (We will explore the astral plane in chapter 6.) They aren't good or bad, just curious. And you can make a decision to not deal with them if you don't want to.

Let's say, for example, that something wakes us up in the middle of the night, and we sense the presence of a being in our room. Most of the time, this startles us and we think, *Oh my gosh, something or someone is here!* Being startled is perfectly natural, so I want you to check in with how you feel *after* the sensation of being startled has passed. Many people have shooed away a perfectly good angel or ancestor spirit because of that initial startled panic they felt. Let the panic settle, and then tune in with your intuition. I can guarantee that if you do this, you will seldom be wrong, just as with living people.

If you have an encounter with a guide that doesn't feel good, I use a three-stage approach to ask spirits to leave. I start by asking politely that the spirit leave. This tends to shoo away the curious, neutral spirits who will sometimes respond with *Ooops, so sorry, I didn't realize you could sense me. Pardon the intrusion...*, and they back away slowly and politely. This will handle the situation most of the time.

If we have the spirit of a stuck dead person (a ghost) or something else that is panicked or needs help, it can be more persistent. It may not just go away when asked nicely. At this point, we need to amp up our power and demand in a firm tone that it leave. I feel my power in my solar plexus energy center, stamp my foot a little, point my finger, and demand that they leave. Try using your "bad dog" voice: "I demand that you leave now!"

If that doesn't work, then we do the spiritual equivalent of calling the cops. We command in the name of a higher power that the spirit leave. This will invoke the spirit of the higher power to help remove the entity, so that it is not just our will against theirs. Commands are very powerful in the spiritual world, but we need some backup here: "I command in the name of Jesus/Allah/Buddha that you leave right now!" This invocation brings spiritual assistance from whoever you call on. Archangel Michael is always a good choice, since he is a warrior angel and protecting humans against spiritual danger is one of his functions. Most of the time, this process will do the trick and clear out any unwanted spirit visitations.

Now let's return to our good spirit guides. Try the guided meditation below to help you meet your spirit guides.

Exercise: Meet Your Guide Meditation

You can download an audio recording of this meditation at http://www.newhar binger.com/50744.

1. Be in a quiet place where you will be undisturbed for a while. Bring your journal with you so you can write down what happens.

2. Begin with the centering, grounding, and protection practices from chapter 2.

3. Now do the basic tuning-in exercise that we covered in chapter 1.

4. From this place of open receptivity, drop your expectations and try to just be present with what comes up.

5. Ask that your guides be present and that they come close to you so you can sense them. Some people ask, "May the highest level guides available to me at this moment come." This screens out the psychic riffraff.

6. Notice what you experience. Extend out your psychic awareness to include all your psychic senses so you are paying attention to how you feel, what you sense, what you know, how your body feels, what you smell or taste, as well as what you might see and hear.

7. Ask your guides this series of questions, but don't get hooked on the answers. You might get some answers and you might not—that is okay. Don't forget that the first thing we get is usually right, even if it's weird. If you have multiple guides, ask the questions of each guide.

   • Do you have a name?

   • What is your function? Are you a healer, protector, my spiritual director, or something else?

   • If it is not clear what type of guide they are, ask this: What type of guide are you—power animal, angel, ancestor, or something else?

   • How have you been communicating with me? Is there is anything I can do to increase the communication?

   • Will you provide me with a sign in the next few days to assure me that you are the real deal?

8. Thank them for coming to you and come back slowly to your body.

9. Breathe any extra energy you have down the grounding cord and move your body around to come back home.

10. Record everything that you experienced in your journal, and use your pendulum to confirm or deny anything that you are not sure about.

Sometimes people will feel a little light-headed after this meditation since it really opens up the upper energy centers like the crown and the brow. Make sure you do some really good grounding after this meditation. Record it in your journal so you don't forget the nuances of it, which tend to slip away quickly after we return to a normal beta level state of consciousness.

I have had many psychic students tell me that "I didn't see anything! I didn't get anything!" after they have done this meditation. But when I ask them what they experienced, I get something like what my friend Edwardo told me.

✳ EDWARDO'S STORY   *Well, I didn't see anything, so I was worried that I was doing it wrong. And then I felt this presence as if someone was standing next to me. I could sense a presence. It was very loving and comforting, and I felt a warm sensation as if this being put its hand on my shoulder. I didn't hear any answers to those questions, but I did know and feel things. I knew it was my grandfather and that he was here to protect me. I could feel how proud he was of me and how much he loves me.*

Edwardo almost fell into the trap of believing he didn't encounter his guide because he didn't see anything, but when he opened up to his other psychic senses, he realized that he got a lot of information.

It's fine to do this meditation as often as you want, and as we go through the upcoming material in the book, we will do variations on this meditation so that you can eventually meet your own team of guides. It's so exciting to be able to communicate directly with our guides, and it can bring so much comfort, healing, and inner guidance to be able to do so.

What's Next?

Now it's time to explore the other dimensions that are available to us as psychics. I am so excited to share with you the map that I have created!

Chapter 6

Explore a Map of the Lower, Middle, and Upper Realms

When we start having psychic experiences, they seem as if they're all random, like a lightbulb suddenly turning on and illuminating a previously dark room. We catch a glimpse of what's in there and then the light turns off, leaving us in darkness again. There seems to be no pattern, no rhyme or reason to it, and this randomness adds to the fear and confusion that many sensitives feel as their gifts awaken.

How much safer and more secure can we feel if we know there is actually a pattern to it all? And there is a pattern that is predictable, relatable, and very useful. Let's go back to the idea of being street smart. If you are street smart, we could plunk you down in any city in the world and if you had the right knowledge, a guide, and a map, you would be able to navigate through that city easily and confidently.

This chapter is where we get the map. It's based on my own years of experience traveling through the psychic realms as well as other metaphysical models including shamanism, the kabbalah, and theosophy. I do want to reiterate that this is a theory, but it's a very useful theory that I have used and taught for decades. It also squares with many other people's psychic experiences of the spiritual realms. I invite you to use it as a guide and also embrace any experiences that you have that might differ from this.

And just a note on terminology: metaphysicians use the terms *realms, worlds, planes, spheres,* and *dimensions* fairly interchangeably. I will stick with "realms" as a grouping of different dimensions.

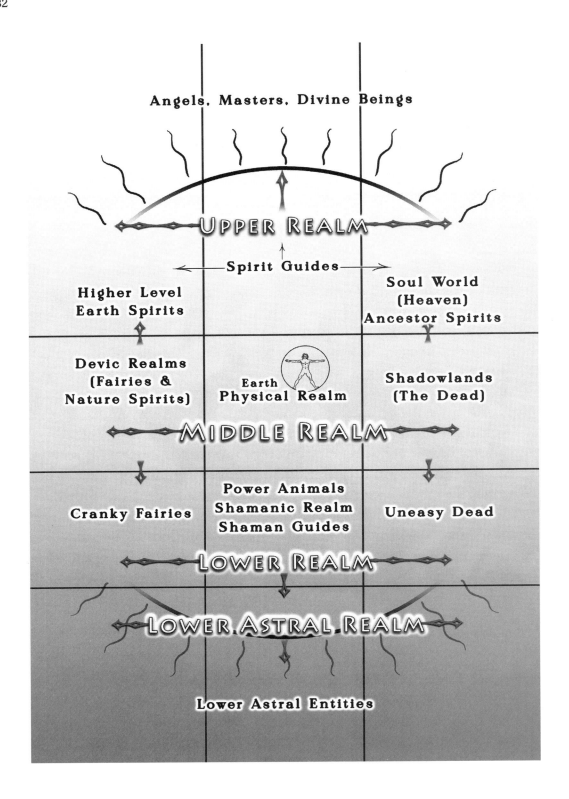

Angels, Masters, Divine Beings

UPPER REALM

Spirit Guides

Higher Level
Earth Spirits

Soul World
(Heaven)
Ancestor Spirits

Devic Realms
(Fairies &
Nature Spirits)

Earth
Physical Realm

Shadowlands
(The Dead)

MIDDLE REALM

Power Animals
Shamanic Realm
Shaman Guides

Cranky Fairies

Uneasy Dead

LOWER REALM

LOWER ASTRAL REALM

Lower Astral Entities

The Map of the Spiritual Realms

I have always found that knowing that there is a structure to the psychic worlds to be quite comforting and empowering. When we first open up, it can seem like our psychic experiences are random and chaotic, like turning on a flashlight and randomly seeing things that are not connected to each other.

This map helps make the connections. As we use this map and take our journey around it, we learn one of the most important psychic skills: discernment. *Discernment* is the ability to tell what kind of spirit or psychic experience you are having, and it creates psychics who are flexible with their knowledge.

Some psychics, like me, are generalists and have the ability to access information from any of these different dimensions, depending on what is needed in the moment. Others have a sweet spot and, for example, feel totally at home with the angels or as mediums. Some psychics have a strong natural connection with the deep and soulful shamanic experiences that we find in the lower realm. Whichever you are, there is something eminently functional about being able to travel through these dimensions at will or at least to recognize them as you have your psychic experiences.

Even if you are not a medium, chances are very good that at some point you may have the opportunity to help someone cross over as an act of service. And as you accumulate experiences in each region of the map, you will build up your ability to discern where you are and what types of spirits are around you.

Laurent was one of my psychic students. He shared his experience with me after having taken my psychic development program.

* LAURENT'S STORY *I felt so much safer and more in control of my psychic experiences. The more I learned and experienced in each realm, the better I could understand and place my own experiences. Then when I would experience something, I knew what it was since I had visited there before. This map brought all the pieces of the puzzle together for me so I could see the big picture, and that took the fear out of it.*

The model that I am sharing with you divides the psychic dimensions into four big realms. If you asked a quantum physicist, they would say that there are really an infinite number of dimensions in this infinite universe that we live in, and I think that is probably true. However, for our purposes, we will narrow this down into the ones that are relevant for us humans that are awakening our psychic abilities.

These are the spiritual realms:

- **The Lower Realm:** Also sometimes known as the shamanic realm, this realm is connected with our subconscious, our dreams, and deep soul work. We can receive soul-level healings by visiting here and connecting with our life's purpose, our past lives, and our future path.

- **The Lower Astral Realm:** This is below the lower realm, and it's considered the bad neighborhood, psychically speaking. Lower astral entities can be tricksters and parasites and are to be avoided. If you stick with the safe psychic practices and avoid the unsafe ones that we discussed in chapter 3, you will be fine.

- **The Middle Realm:** Occupying planet Earth, this realm has two different sides. One side includes people and the human world. The other side contains the spirits of the natural world, including the spiritual essences of plants (otherwise known as "fairies") and all the other spirits of the natural world.

- **The Upper Realm:** Included in this realm are beings of higher consciousness such as angels, the ascended masters, prophets and saints, and other beings of pure consciousness. This is also where we find soul world (aka heaven), which is where our souls go when they are not here

We will spend the remaining chapters of this book diving into each of these realms, but I wanted to give you the big picture right now. It's important to keep in mind that these realms are dimensions of reality beyond what humans can perceive with our five senses. We know scientifically that there are ranges of light and color—like infrared and ultraviolet—that exist beyond those that we can perceive with our physical eye. We know this because we have created scientific instruments that are capable of registering these light frequencies. And yet, though we cannot see them with our physical eye, we perceive these dimensions with our psychic senses, and the more we open up our psychic senses, the more of these other dimensions we can experience.

These different dimensions coexist simultaneously alongside ours, each one at a slightly different frequency, much like ultraviolet is a different frequency than what we can perceive in the visible light spectrum. Much as each color of light is a different frequency and vibration, each of these dimensions has its own frequency too.

Earth is a fairly dense frequency, which makes it both an interesting and challenging dimension to incarnate into. We might use the piano keyboard as a good analogy.

If we place Earth at middle C, we can drop frequency and go for lower notes down the keyboard. In our case, we only go one note down into the lower (or shamanic) realm. It's important to note that this is not a bad or evil place, and it's nothing to fear—it's not hell or any such place. However, if you dropped far enough down the keyboard, you might find some pretty uncomfortable dimensions down there.

We can also go up the piano keyboard with each note taking us to a higher dimension. This piano analogy breaks down at this point, since we also need to be able to travel sideways through these dimensions as you can see in figure 3. These other dimensions exist alongside ours, and as psychics, we learn to perceive and gather information from these other dimensions. I have simplified this map into a two-dimensional thing, but like any map, it represents something more complex. The dimensions are more like those Russian nesting dolls, with each one surrounding another one, or as the quantum theorists say, like bubbles that exist next to each other and sometimes touch each other but are separated from each other by a barrier.

The Veils Between Dimensions

These barriers, also known as *veils*, separate these dimensions from each other, rather like the membrane of a cell helps to contain what is inside that cell. Frequently, we will have a psychic experience because the veil between one dimension and another becomes very thin, and it's possible to perceive through or even pass through these veils. For instance, an uneasy spirit of the dead, otherwise known as a ghost, can pass through these veils and appear in our dimension in a way that people can perceive them.

There are times of the day and times of the year when the veils become thin, and it's easier to perceive things from the other side of the veil. At Halloween, the veil between our world and the dimension of the uneasy dead, sometimes called the *shadowlands*, becomes very thin, and we can communicate more easily with the departed. On May 1st (at least here in the Northern Hemisphere, where I live), the veil between our world and the world of the fairies becomes thin, and people have more experiences with nature spirits.

At certain times of the day this happens too. The fairy realms are closer to us at dawn and dusk, but 3 a.m. is the time of day when the dimension of the departed is closer. People who work in hospitals know that more people die during this "witching" hour than at other times, and many people also have strong psychic connections to their departed loved ones at this time.

Some physical locations are places where the veils between worlds are naturally thinner, and we can perceive across dimensions. There is a theory that the big megalithic structures like the pyramids, Stonehenge, other stone circles were placed intentionally on these spots to take advantage of these soft spots between dimensions.

People who study paranormal phenomenon such as UFOs and cryptozoology (creatures like the Yeti and the Loch Ness monster) theorize that those are other dimensional beings who find their way here, at least temporarily, through portals or gaps in the veils. They also find their way back again, which is why no one has yet found the body of Big Foot anywhere. If we walk through the woods and spot something otherworldly, it might be because we have stumbled into a situation where two dimensions briefly collide and we can experience the apparition of a ghost, a UFO, or a cryptid for a few moments. I am not sure if this true, but I do think it's an interesting theory.

We must also be careful not to open up portals between dimensions, or at least if we do, we must have sense enough to close them again. Tools such as the Ouija board are notorious for opening up a doorway between dimensions, in this case the lower astral realm, which is where many lower vibration entities exist. Many unpleasant, scary, and unnecessary hauntings happen because repeated use of such tools opens this doorway over and over again, reinforcing it and making it difficult to close.

Let's take a minute to explore one of these dimensions—the astral dimension—in particular. We'll see how it presents both an opportunity and a challenge to developing psychics.

The Astral Dimension

The astral dimension is just one dimension away from our earthly dimension, so we have many opportunities to be in contact with it, especially as we are opening up to our psychic abilities You can think about the astral dimension as the egg white that surrounds the egg yolk in a hard-boiled egg, with the egg yolk being our human dimension. Or maybe think of it as a set of nesting Russian dolls.

There are three levels to the astral dimension: the upper, middle, and lower astral realms. As psychics, we experience these differently. All of the levels of the astral dimensions are interesting places to be, but, for the most part, we need to bypass this dimension when possible.

The upper astral realm is very connected to our dream world; it's full of archetypal beings and mystical beasts, and it can be a fun place to visit. If you have ever had a dream where you are flying, you were probably experiencing moving through the upper astral realm since this is where people go when they experience something called *astral projection*. This occurs when our astral, or spirit, body leaves our physical body and we visit this upper astral realm. Sometimes we meet our spirit guides here; it's a like a neutral meeting ground for spirit beings.

The middle part of the astral realm—the haunt, if you will excuse the pun, of the uneasy spirits of the dead, otherwise known as ghosts—is the shadowlands. Mediums learn to access this dimension to help those lost souls find their way home to heaven.

The lower astral realm is a darker and trickier place and is worthy of discussion before we move on. It's lower down in frequency that any place we want to visit as psychics and is below the "lower realm" on our map. I want to make you aware of some of the pitfalls of experiencing the lower astral realm, since new psychics often encounter this place as we are opening up and learning. The lower astral realm is full of trouble for those of us who are sensitives. The entities that exist there are not favorably inclined to humans and are often either parasitic beings who attach to us for the purposes of taking our life-force energy, or they are more malevolent trickster entities who love to fool and manipulate people.

Please avoid the following psychic practices unless you have had detailed training with someone else who really knows what they are doing:

- séances with the Ouija board or other spirit boards (actually, really *never* do this)

- table tipping

- astral projection on purpose (rather than naturally in a dream)

- EVP (electronic voice phenomenon), if done over and over again in the same place

- summoning spirit spells or rituals, which are easily found on the internet these days

Particularly problematic is the Ouija board, just because it's so available and found in the game section of toy stores. I am sure many of us have played around with it. I certainly did in my teenage years, down in the basement of someone's house during a high school slumber party. Playing with it seems like harmless but titillating fun.

However, there are many documented and even more anecdotal cases of naïve psychic students who connect with one of these lower astral beings in Ouija board sessions. Unfortunately, they can be notoriously malicious and difficult to get rid of.

Lower astral beings are shape-shifter spirits who don't speak the truth about who they are and will present you a face that you are familiar with. They are happy to tell you that they are the poor and pathetic ghost of a lost child, or Jesus or Archangel Michael, usually with the purpose of gaining your trust so that they can later manipulate you; this is why they are sometimes called the *face changers*. You can tell the difference between a lower astral entity and a true guide by how they speak to you, what they offer, and if they criticize or threaten you. Also use your basic discernment skills here; lower astral beings will feel icky even if they tell you that they are benevolent. These beings are the cause of many hauntings, especially the scarier and more dangerous ones like poltergeist spirits, and the other hauntings we see in horror movies. Actually, when someone thinks they have a "demon," it's often one of these beings.

PSYCHIC TIP: *Recognizing the Lower Astral Entities*

A truly beneficial guide will never promise you riches, health, or fame, and they won't flatter you. They don't ever criticize, shame, blame, or threaten you either. Lower astral entities will flatter you and promise you the world—until you question them, and then they can become nasty, mean, and threatening. If you have connected to a lower astral entity, stop all contact with them immediately and use the techniques we learned in chapter 2 to remove them. If that doesn't work, call in a professional psychic who can help you.

One of the other high-risk practices that we want to avoid, unless you are highly trained in it, is *astral projection*. The concept here is that there is part of our being referred to as the *astral body* that can leave our physical body and roam around through the astral dimension. Also known as an out-of-body experience, or an OBE, the hallmark of this experience is the feeling of flying or floating above your body, and even being able to see your body, while your consciousness hovers outside it. Many people do this quite naturally while they are sleeping, and these natural occurrences are fairly harmless. I do not advise, however, attempting to do astral projection intentionally unless you receive training from an expert, since it's very common to find yourself in some of the unsavory neighborhoods of the lower astral dimension.

The risk of this is twofold. On one hand, we may possibly open portals in our home by repeated astral travel. On the other hand, many astral projectors bring back astral entities with them on their return. I put astral projection into the same high-risk category as ghostbusting and holding séances; these are fine for the highly trained and potentially dangerous for the newbies.

If you are someone who naturally astral travels, and many psychics do, please get further training in it. I highly recommend the work of Robert Bruce and his informative book *Astral Dynamics: The Complete Book of Out-of-Body Experiences.*[11]

Psychics who are still learning often encounter the astral dimension, which is why it's important to discuss it. We need to learn to raise our frequency enough to pass through this realm and connect with higher-level beings. As we go through the rest of our work together, I will teach you some easy and effective ways to bypass the astral realm and go straight to the good stuff.

The Inner Sanctuary

If we don't want to encounter the astral dimension, where then do we go? I am going to give you a safe place to land: your *inner sanctuary.* This place, which exists inside you, functions as our stepping-off place into the other dimensions that we will be exploring. Think of it as the waiting room in a train station or an airport. It's a safe zone that has connecting points to all the other dimensions that we will visit. Your inner sanctuary will be unique to you, and as you visit your inner sanctuary, it might change over time. Many people find that their inner sanctuary expands and gives them more and more access points to other psychic dimensions as their skills grow. It might be a place that you have been before, or it might be somewhere conjured up by your psyche. It can be inside a building, like a church or a temple. It might be really familiar, like a room in your house. Or it might be located outside, like a beach, or a grove of trees, or a beautiful meadow.

Your inner sanctuary is a wonderful place to practice opening up your psychic senses and also to meet your guides. Let's explore yours right now. Remember you can't do this wrong or make a mistake with it. You will experience something, and whatever happens is just right for this moment. Drop your expectations, relax, and see if you can be present with whatever is happening in the moment.

Exercise: Inner Sanctuary Meditation

Settle into a comfortable place and have your psychic journal nearby. (You can download an audio recording of this meditation at http://www.newharbinger.com/50744.)

1. Begin with centering, grounding, and protecting yourself.

2. Set the intention to visit your inner sanctuary. It can help to speak this out loud: "I am opening up my psychic senses so that I can visit my inner sanctuary right now."

3. Is there anything to see? Look down at the ground and your feet. Pick your gaze up and look all around you. What is there to see?

4. What do you know about where you are? You might just notice that you are at the beach or in a temple on a mountaintop. Expand your knowing by asking yourself, *What do I know about this place?*

5. Do you hear anything? You might hear the sound of a crackling fire or waves crashing on a beach.

6. Can you smell or taste anything, like the smell of incense in a church or pine needles if you are in the woods?

7. What do you feel in your body? Can you feel the sun, warm on your skin, or is there anything to touch there? And how are your emotions? Do you feel peaceful, happy, and contented? Or do you feel nervous and excited?

8. Spend some time exploring this place. When you are ready, come back into your body by taking a deep breath and releasing any extra energy back down through your feet and into the earth. Wiggle your fingers and toes, and open your eyes.

Do this meditation regularly to strengthen your psychic senses. Don't be surprised if your guides show up in your inner sanctuary: this is a wonderful place to connect with them.

What's Next?

And now let's dive into our exploration of the first of these realms, the lower realm. There is much power and healing to be experienced in the lower realm: many people have spontaneous healings, remember their past lives, and get crucial information regarding their life purpose here.

Chapter 7

Heal with Shaman Guides
and Power Animals

The lower realm is a deep, rich, and fascinating psychic dimension. Some of my very first training as a psychic was with a shaman, so I have a strong connection and appreciation for this realm. It is also sometimes called the shamanic realm, and the first thing to know about it is that even though it is called the "lower" realm, it is not some hell dimension, nor is it connected to anything evil or bad.

And yet it is not always a comfortable place for all psychic travelers. In the lower realm, we have the chance to encounter a deeper level of ourselves than we get in our ordinary life. The lower realm is connected to our subconscious self, our inner shadow, and our dreams.

Spiritual work and psychic work are not always all rainbows, unicorns, and fairy dust (although those are fun too). Sometimes we need to tap into the deeper, darker, unhealed parts of ourselves, and the lower realm allows us to access the subconscious part of ourselves, much like exploring our dreams does. Learning how to navigate the lower realm is much like doing dream interpretation, and if you have been recording and considering your dreams as we learned in chapter 4, you will have a good start at understanding your lower realm experiences.

And more than any other psychic dimension, journeying through the lower realm gives us direct connection to our own soul and all the wisdom that holds for us. Many psychic students have spontaneous past life memories when visiting the lower realm and get vital information about their life's purpose. I frequently receive healings when I visit this place, which I do spontaneously every time I have a big transition or rite of passage in my own life. And in the lower realm, we are invited to confront our fears, break through emotional blocks, and make peace with our own inner shadow self.

It reminds me of one of my favorite scenes in the Star Wars movie *The Empire Strikes Back*. In this scene, Luke is doing his Jedi training and Master Yoda takes Luke to a cave as a test and to help Luke meet his own shadow self. When Luke asks what is in the cave, Yoda says, "Only what you take with you."

Of course, the famous scene ends with Luke seeing Darth Vader and they duel. When Luke wins the duel, he realizes he has been fighting himself, or at least his own dark side. George Lucas was a student of the great Joseph Campbell, who worked with archetypes and the concept of the hero's journey, which Lucas used to make the story of Luke so poignant to many of us. Keep this in mind, since when we travel to the lower realm, we will be going on the same kind of inner journey, only maybe not with light sabers.

The lower realm is reached with our intention and imagination by allowing ourselves to fall through a hole, Alice in Wonderland–style, or by going through a cave, just like Luke did. In fact, the story of Alice in Wonderland is a fantastic shamanic, lower realm experience, and it's quite possible that Lewis Carroll had a lower realm journey to inspire such a story. The hole, cave, or passageway represents the shift from one dimension to another; it is the entry point into the lower realm. We will find and visit this entry point inside your inner sanctuary, and when we get there, you will most likely meet your shamanic guides.

Your Shamanic Guides

These spirit beings are the denizens of the lower realm and are here to guide, protect, and even heal us. It's very important to release our expectations of these guides, to relax and let go of fear since they can be a bit intense, and to remember that there is nothing dark down there, except, as Luke learned, what we bring there ourselves.

Human Spirits and Mythic Creatures

Upon entering the lower realm, most people will be met by a spirit guide whose job it is to lead them along the right pathways in the lower realm, much like Alice's white rabbit. It's very common to meet mythical creatures—like dragons, unicorns, and other strange beasts—as guides to the lower realm. It's an important situation to practice the skill of discernment, since things are not always what they seem in the lower realm. Fierce mythic beasts or funky-looking guides may well have wisdom, compassion, and important guidance for you. You might be startled by what you encounter, but, of course, if anything ever really feels off, negative, or creepy, use your banishing skills to get rid of it.

One of my most powerful shamanic guides is a being called the Bone Woman. I met her many years ago on one of my very first shamanic journeys. I found myself in a cave with a big bonfire burning in the middle of it. Next to the fire sat an old, naked woman who wore a skirt made of bones. She was covered in tattoos and her teeth were dyed black, which I found out when she smiled at me. She was fierce and intimidating, so I said something like "Woah! ... Hello?"

Then she hit me over the head with a big bone, laughing while she did it. She told me that was to open up my crown chakra and bring my psychic senses more fully online. It reminded me of how you used to hit a TV to try to get better reception, way back in the day. "You look, but you do not see," she told me that day.

The Bone Woman said that she was a truth speaker and an oracle, and would answer any question that I had as long as I was prepared to hear the truth. I have worked with her many times in the past thirty years, and I always cringe a little when I encounter her, since the truth is often hard to bear.

"Is this the right relationship for me?" I once asked her timidly, already knowing and fearing the answer.

Whack! "Open up your eyes and really see! What do you see?" she said, hitting me, as usual, with her bone. Then suddenly, I could see the truths behind the illusions of the relationship, all the red flags showing up, and my heart breaking a little as I let go of the fantasy of the happy ever after. Then she held me as I cried that one out. She then did a beautiful heart healing, since her hard truths are always followed by much compassion, love, and healing.

Besides human spirits and mythic creatures, almost everyone will encounter spirit guides in the form of animals in the lower realm. In shamanic circles, we call them *power animals,* since their function is to help us find our power, or to lend us theirs.

Power Animals

It's so fun, easy, and satisfying to connect with our power animals. The spirit essence of animals helps us connect with the qualities, or the essence, of what those animals represent to us. We all know that lions represent the quality of courage, and we say someone is as loyal as a dog or as clever as a monkey. When we encounter power animals, we are able to connect with those qualities in ourself. When animals come to us as psychic messengers, they may be bringing us this essential quality that we need to embody, or they might point out the qualities that we are lacking in the moment but that we really need. In Native American shamanism, this potent energy that power animals bring to us is called their *medicine.*

I have a strong connection to mouse as a power animal. The medicine of mouse is all about paying attention to the details of things, which is not my strongest suit. When mouse shows up in my dreams, meditations, or, in fact, my life, I know it's a message that I need to check the details and make sure that I haven't dropped the ball somewhere. Mouse reminds me that the devil is in the details.

We all have a wide variety of power animals. We may—or may not—encounter these animals in the physical terrain around us. My student Star told me this beautiful story about her power animal.

✳ STAR'S STORY *Deer are such a strong guide for me. I live in New England, so there are a lot of deer around, but I know when I see one, there is probably a message for me. One day when I was house hunting with my partner and our daughter, we arrived at a house and three deer were standing in the driveway. It was a little deer family, and I felt like they were welcoming us home. Even though there was a fierce bidding war on the house, I knew we were going to get it, and we did. It was our house and the deer sent the message that all would be well.*

Of course, we may have power animals that do not live in our neck of the woods, and if so, we need to pay attention to all the places that they might show up in our lives. Perhaps they frequent our dreams, meditations, or visions. Or we might encounter them as stuffed animals in shops, see them on TV, or encounter them as images that we see when we are out and about. We might collect images of these animals, or get tattoos of them. Have you ever become slightly obsessed with a specific animal? If so, then you see them everywhere, right?

My daughter connects to hummingbirds, whose meaning is all about helping us find a joy-filled path in life. When she was in the midst of some hard decisions about her life, she received a package in the mail. One of her friends, who is an artist, painted a picture of a hummingbird and sent it to her. Her friend listened to a hunch, a well-timed psychic insight, that my daughter needed a sign and that was it. This sign helped her make a decision to pick a more challenging but potentially more joy-filled path for herself.

We are best served by being humble with and curious about power animals. Sometimes big power comes in little packages, such as insects. Don't be disappointed if you get an ant or a lowly worm. The ant is one of the strongest creatures in the planet, capable of lifting many times its own weight. Ant medicine can help you carry the heavy burdens in your life or remind you how strong you really are.

The humble earthworm is helpful when we need to be grounded and do deep healing from the past. Worms are magic at creating the garden's gold of compost from old refuse and are a sign that you are finding nourishment and growth from clearing the past.

It's very common to have a power animal that you are afraid of in real life. Things like snakes and spiders make fantastic power animals, even if we are afraid of the real creature. The gift of the snake is about the transformation that comes about through mystical knowledge, and spiders are the patron power animal of writers and can help us find the words to tell our stories. We may not want to cuddle with our power animals in our actual life and that's okay, but we do benefit greatly from staying open to their messages.

It's considered bad form to shoo away your power animal just because you think it's yucky. Please don't stomp on the ant or the worm that shows up for you, or try to punch it in the nose as one of my students did when he saw a shark as a power animal in a meditation. "I panicked!" he told me after his first shamanic journey. "I am terrified of sharks, and I had heard that they go away if you punch them in the nose." It took him a while to come to terms with the gift of this shark, but eventually he came to appreciate the power the shark was bringing him, which was the laser focus, concentration, and single-minded determination to grab on to what we want in life and not let go of it.

This is a good time to practice relaxing our expectations and just showing up for what is happening. It's all too easy to decide beforehand what you want to experience and then try to force having your expectations met. Having strong expectations in the first place is a sure sign that your mind is making up the experience rather than you having a real psychic connection to your guides.

My friend Gabriella loves cats more than anything, and when she first tried to connect to her power animals, she was sure that she was going to see a cat. She was shocked and a little sad when she saw a weasel instead. She wondered to herself, *Where is my cat?* and thought, *I hate weasels. Go away, you creepy weasel! Here, kitty, kitty...* Try as she might, she could not make the reviled weasel go away or the admired cat appear.

This was an excellent sign that it was a true psychic hit rather than just something that she was making up in her own head, since real psychic hits come on their own, sometimes contrary to what our minds expect. When Gabriella looked up the meaning of weasel, it perfectly fit what she needed in the moment, since weasel medicine brings us better self-esteem and a sense of our own charisma. Weasel is genius in discerning when someone is lying or being sneaky. Weasel always knows what's true and what's a lie, and this was just what Gabriella needed.

Sometimes power animals pass their blessings on to us in strange ways. Don't freak out if your power animal bites or even eats you in a shamanic journey. If they bite us, they are transferring their power to us. Shortly before I learned the energy healing modality of Reiki, I had a dream that two cobras bit the palms of my hands. Cobras represent the kundalini energy, the awakened life-force energy that precedes spiritual awakening. When they bit my palms, I knew they were transferring their power to my hands and helping me begin my journey as an energy healer.

Sometimes shamanic journeys include an initiation, often in the form of the shamanic death. My student Amber told me about a shamanic journey that she did in South America.

✳ AMBER'S STORY *It was a very intense and very authentic journey that went all through the night. Sometime in the middle in the night, I had a vision where jaguar came and ate me. I felt no pain or fear; I knew this power animal was helping me dissolve my former self and assisting me in letting go of my past. When I came out of the journey in the morning, I felt like a new person and much in my life changed after that.*

Amber experienced a true initiation, the shamanic death. Most of the time however, working with power animals is fun and easy. They make joyful and supportive guides on our journey through life.

Once we have had a power animal sighting, how do we know what it means? It takes some research to understand all the meanings of these animals. The easiest thing to do is to research them online. If you Google the name of the animal—something like, "whale power animal"—you will get lots of immediate information on what that might mean for you.

There are also many excellent books about power animals. If this whole topic resonates with you, I highly recommend that you get one of these books as a reference to keep on hand. I love *Shamanic Power Animals: Embracing the Teachings of Our Non-Human Friends*[12] by Don José Ruiz, as well as the works of Steven Farmer and Ted Andrews. I love *Messages from Your Animal Spirit Guides Oracle Cards: A 44-Card Deck and Guidebook*[13] by Steven Farmer, and there are many other animal card decks that are wonderful too. If you want to deeply understand power animals, the card decks are a must-have tool. Once you have a book or two and a pack of these power animal oracle cards, you can look up the meanings of the animals when you perceive them.

Tips for Working with Power Animals

As with all of our guides, our connection with our power animals grows with time and attention. Here are some good ways to honor and strengthen that connection.

- ❁ Set your intention to meet your power animal. You can write down the request in your journal or speak it out loud.

- ❁ Then pay attention to what animals show up in your dreams, meditations, and journeys. Or you might see them in your daily life.

- ❁ Watch for animal behavior that is outside the normal, such as the hawk sitting on the roof of your car every morning for days.

- ❁ Do the shamanic journey listed below and see which animals show up.

- ❁ Get a deck of power animal oracle/medicine cards and add them into your daily card pulls. Referring to the reference books that come with the card decks can be very helpful in learning about power animals and understanding their medicine.

- ❁ Notice what animals do in your daily life, especially if they act in an unusual way that you feel is a sign.

- ❁ Once you have met a power animal, find a way to honor it in your life. Get a picture or a little statue of your power animal so you can look at it. Learn everything you can about that animal's behavior and also their medicine.

- ❁ Get in the habit of thanking your power animals when they do show up with guidance and medicine for you.

And, of course, keep track of your experiences with power animals in your psychic journal.

The most likely place to meet a power animal is in doing a shamanic journey. Let's discuss that next.

The Shamanic Journey

To visit the lower realm, we will be doing a specific type of meditation called the shamanic journey. Traditionally, this type of meditation is done to sounds of fast-paced, loud drumming. The noise of the drumming interrupts our thinking and is wonderful for people who are overthinkers and who struggle with shutting off their minds when they meditate. Drumming tends to turn off the mind and put you very quickly into a trance state in the low alpha brain wave. I have easily found this type of drumming, often called drum journeys, on YouTube. It's a fast drumbeat and it can take a little bit to get used to it. Most drum-assisted shamanic journeys are about thirty minutes long. When the drumming changes to a much faster tempo, it's time to return to the ordinary world.

When the drumming starts, you will bring yourself to your inner sanctuary as we learned to do in chapter 6. Once you are in your inner sanctuary, look around for the entrance to a cave or maybe a hole in the ground, if you want to go Alice in Wonderland style. The entrance to the shamanic realm can also be found at the edges of things, like the edge between the land and the sea, maybe behind a waterfall, or down the trunk of a hollow tree. Try not to overthink it, set your intention to visit the lower world, and then look for a way to get there. Some people fall down a rabbit hole, drop down through an old hollow tree, enter though a doorway in a rock wall, or even jump into a pool of water. Stay loose with it and see what happens.

Once you allow yourself to walk into the cave or fall down the hole, there is usually a little transitional space. It's like walking through a dark tunnel, and soon thereafter, you are in the lower realm.

Once there, look around for a guide whose function is to escort you through this realm. It might be a power animal, but it could be a more human-type guide. One of my psychic students who was feeling some trepidation about this journey was met by a very friendly ladybug, and after that, she knew everything would be okay.

Whether you meet a guide right away or not, just start exploring this realm. It's very normal for you to arrive somewhere out in the open, even though you went through a cave, much like Alice did in Wonderland. You could find yourself at a beach, in a lush jungle, or pretty much anywhere. It's hard to say what can happen in the shamanic journey, since it's such an individual experience. It also differs every time you go. You might have a healing experience such as being led to a pool to wash away your cares. You might perceive glimpses of past lives or get useful information about what your life purpose is. Or you might just hang around for a while with not much happening until the drums call you back.

Ultimately journeying though the lower realm is about reconnecting to our spiritual power and reclaiming lost parts of ourselves. Sometimes it's about spiritual initiations, and these experiences transform who we are in very primal ways. Because of this potential to reclaim our power, things can seem a little intense. If they do, try to relax and understand we might need healing to really claim our power, or we might need to be confronted with lost, shadow parts of ourselves.

Siobhan told me about her excitement and nervousness about her journey. She suffers from chronic pain and said that her life changed significantly after her journey.

✳ SIOBHAN'S STORY *I was really excited about this journey and also a little bit nervous. I looked for a rabbit hole or a cave, and didn't see anything, but I was drawn to the edge of a lake. As I waded through the lake, a mermaid took me all the way under the water. It was delightful. We swam all around and eventually landed on the shore of an island. It was like a beautiful garden, and although I wandered around for quite a while, looking at the plants and creatures there, nothing really dramatic happened, or so I thought. I felt so peaceful and calm. The mermaid took me to a healing pool and a dragonfly landed on my hand.*

After the journey, I had way less pain than I normally do, and I had asked for clarity about my marriage. When I looked up the medicine that dragonfly offers, it's all about letting go of illusions and seeing the truth about things. I became very clear about what I wanted in my marriage and was able to renegotiate my needs in a way that gave the marriage a new life.

Siobhan does weekly shamanic journeys as a way to stay in touch with herself and her guides. She says that this practice has changed her life: she experienced a gentle healing that accrued over time. My student Tai told me about a much more intense initiation that they received during their journey.

✸ TAI'S STORY *I slid down a slide into a deep cave, which was sort of fun. Once I got there, however, I felt overwhelmed by fear. I was met by a guide, a fierce warrior with a big, sharp spear and lots of tattoos and paint on his body. He led me through a jungle until we got to a clearing with a huge bonfire in the middle of it. Next to the bonfire was an old medicine man who told me that if I wanted to move forward in my life, I had to face my fears. He said I needed to jump into the fire and let it burn away my past. I was badly burned as a child and am terrified of fire; I didn't want to do it. The medicine man explained that I was at a crossroad in my life but that no one could make the decision for me.*

Eventually I just did it. I jumped into the fire, since I knew he was right. Once I was in the fire, it just felt warm and soft and did not burn or hurt at all. I cried and released a lot of fear and pain from my past. The medicine man told me that I had a past life where I had burned to death. When I came out of the fire, I felt clean, strong, and new, and something deep in me had healed.

Tai experienced many changes in their life after this experience. Some aspects of their life that had been stuck began to move forward, and they felt powerful and able to create their life on their own terms.

The next step is to experience your own shamanic journey. The exercise below will guide you on your journey.

Exercise: The Shamanic Journey

Prepare for this experience by making sure you have some quiet, alone time and finding a shamanic drum journey recording on YouTube. Lie down in a comfortable place and have your journal nearby to record your experience. (You can download an audio recording of this meditation at http://www.newharbinger.com/50744.)

1. Start the drum recording and lie down. It's fine to have an intention for your journey, or you can just set the intention to explore the lower realm and meet your shamanic guides.

2. Begin by doing your basic centering, grounding, and protecting meditation.

3. Imagine that you are in your inner sanctuary. Take a few moments to open up your psychic senses by noting what you can see, hear, know, taste, smell, or feel about your inner sanctuary.

4. Look around your inner sanctuary for the entrance to the lower realm. It might be a cave, a rabbit hole, a hollow tree trunk, or behind a waterfall.

5. Once you arrive in the lower realm, look around for a guide to help you navigate. If one doesn't show up right away, you can request one. Remember to stay open about what form this guide might take. If you don't see a guide, you can start exploring on your own.

6. Explore the realm and see what happens. Of all the realms that we visit, this is the best place to drop your expectations and bring your full attention to what is happening in the moment. If you can, be open to it all without fear or judgment.

7. When the drumming increases its tempo, it's time to return to your inner sanctuary. Ask your guide to bring you back to the cave, hole, or opening that you came through and intend to return to yourself. Don't forget to thank your guide.

8. Once you are back in the inner sanctuary, begin to come back to your body in the real world. Wiggle your fingers and toes, take a few deep breaths and bring yourself back.

It can take a few minutes to readjust to being in the real world and back in your body. Write everything you experienced down while it's still fresh in your mind.

Once you have done your journey and recorded it in your journal, it might take a little bit of effort to find the meaning in it all. Look up the medicine of any power animals that you perceived on your journey. You can also use a dream dictionary to decode anything that happened that might be symbolic in nature. Interpreting the experience as if it were a dream can help you find meaning in the symbolic and ritualistic things that happen in this kind of journey.

Also remember that your personal symbols library always trumps the collective symbols library, so it's wise to continue asking yourself, *What does that mean to me?*

Here are a few things to try if you struggle with this type of meditation. Some people can't get past the drums and find them too jarring. Try regular music or even some crystal bowl music rather than the drums. If you are more attuned to the upper realm, the crystal bowls will help you get there.

Many people have a better result when they try this meditation when they are outside and lying on the ground. You might try it at night rather than the day; it works very well in the small hours of the morning, between midnight and dawn. Don't be afraid to experiment and modify this journey to find something that works for you.

And it might just not be for you. If so, that is okay. Simply move on to the next chapter. Remember that every psychic has a sweet spot on the map that corresponds with their natural psychic skill set and the purpose for which those skills are meant to be used.

What's Next?

Now we will leave the lower realm and explore the middle realm. We will start with the beautiful world of nature spirits, including fairies and elementals. This is a very delightful and curious psychic dimension where we really need to understand the rules—otherwise, we might find these beings a little mischievous if we don't pay our respects.

Chapter 8

Commune with Spirits of the Natural World

The middle realm is the psychic dimension that coexists with our dimensions right here on planet Earth. It's made up of two parts, both of which we will explore. The first part is the spirits of the natural world, which we will discuss in this chapter. The second part of the middle realm holds those people that have passed away but haven't fully moved on yet; those are the wayward spirits that we call ghosts. In chapter 9, we will talk about what happens when you die, why some people get stuck, and how we can help them move on. This is a fascinating topic, but for now, let's jump into the world of nature spirits.

Some of my earliest psychic experiences were with the nature spirits. One summer when I was still a small child, I remember visiting my grandparents' lakeside cabin in Vermont. One day I was just daydreaming and looking at the forest and the lake, and suddenly I could see a pulsing glow around all the trees and plants. I was perceiving energy that was connecting all the living things in a glowing web of light. I knew somehow that plants were more alive and conscious than most people thought they were, that they were all connected and somehow communicated with each other. I remember telling some adult that the trees whispered to each other and was again told about how vivid my imagination was.

At dusk on that same day, I asked my grandmother what all the little dancing blue lights were—they looked like fireflies, but they were bigger and blue. She looked around, and although I knew that she wasn't seeing what I was seeing, I also knew that she believed me. "Those are fairies," she told me. "They like to come out at dusk and dawn, and you are lucky that you can see them. Not many people can."

The word "fairies" conjures up images like Tinkerbell or little Victorian girls with nightdresses and wings, but the world of the fae is diverse, a little intense, and not at all like the Disney images that we all grew up with. ("Fae" is a Celtic word that means the fairy folk.) Every living thing and all the different parts of nature—trees, rocks, bodies of water, and mountains, as well as every individual plant and flower—have a spiritual essence to them. Each is not only alive and interconnected to every other living thing, but it also has its own unique spiritual essence that we can perceive and relate to.

The most important thing to consider as we explore this psychic dimension is that the world of the fae has its own set of rules that we need to be cognizant of. Nature spirits can be friendly and aligned with humans or not, mostly depending on the level of respect that we offer to the earth—and sadly these days, there is no longer much respect for Mother Earth and her creatures.

These nature spirits are aligned with the wild energy that we recognize as the circle of life. Nature spirits are very rarely evil, but they are not always beneficial to humans either. A shark is not evil if it takes a bite out of you; it's just doing its own thing in that circle of life. This wild, natural energy does not obey the human rules of right and wrong. The shark doesn't eat the bad people and avoid the good people. It probably thinks you look like a tasty seal, and the only way to tell the difference between a nasty-tasting human and a delicious seal is to take a little nibble and find out what you taste like on the inside. Nothing personal at all, it's the circle of life, right?

And yet, we can break down these spirits into three different categories: those that are benevolent, neutral, or actively malevolent toward humans. Most of the time, you will encounter the benevolent and neutral spirits, so there isn't much to worry about. However, even the best of the fae can have a mischievous side to them, and if you are disrespectful, they can be vengeful. Let's dig a little more into who the fae are and how we can learn to play by their rules.

The Fae

In times when humans had a much closer relationship to the earth and earth spirits, there was a stronger belief in the fairy folk. These beings were tricksters who might steal a child from their crib and replace it with a changeling, one of their own—at least according to the superstitious beliefs used to account for infant deaths and diseases. Or maybe the fae would draw you into a stone circle, which is the gateway to their hidden realm. You would hear their haunting music, see their sparking lights, and feel the seduction of their charm and fairy gold. Since time passes at a different rate in fairy world, you might return a day later to find that twenty years had passed in the human realm. These are some of the old folk tales about the fairy folk.

According to these superstitions, if you are a good steward of the land and are kind to and respectful of the fae, they will be helpful allies. At all costs, one must not cut down their sacred trees, and one must be careful not to wander into the stone circles and burrows on certain nights of the year. The fae are known to be fond of music, sweets, and shiny things, and therefore they appreciate offerings of this type. According to the legends, if you are not respectful, they will sour your milk, blight your crops, and even steal your children.

When I first started working with the spirits of the natural world, I was expecting the tall, stately elves from *Lord of the Rings.* What I discovered was a vast array of many different types of spirits that occupy this part of the middle realm. They are often strange looking and hardly ever look human, although most fall into a human-ish sort of look. They are many types of the fae, including what we call pixies, fairies, brownies, gnomes, and trolls. There are naiads, the spirits of water, and dryads, the spirits of trees. These are, generally speaking, the spirit essences of plants, minerals, and the elements. They can be individual spirits that inhabit one particular plant, like the dryads, or they might be quite large spirits, called the *devas,* which are more like shepherds, in charge of caretaking a whole mountain, a valley, or a body of water. I have seen a deva as a huge energy moving through a large, ancient forest, very untouched by humans, and was told by my shaman friend that this was the local forest spirit. It would help and protect us if we made the proper offerings of respect—or potentially kick us off the mountain if we didn't.

We live alongside this realm, and as we discussed in chapter 6, there are certain times of the day and the year as well as certain places where our world and the fairy world connect. Fairies love the edges of things, so we encounter them more easily at dawn and dusk, at the edge of water and the land, and at the edge of the forest and the meadow.

PSYCHIC TIP: *Inviting in the Fairies*

May Day, the first of May, is the day when the veil between the world of humans and the fae is the thinnest. It is a very good day to encounter the spirits of nature. Try a ritual to honor them by leaving some milk and honey and maybe a few shiny things for them, and do something to tend the land. Plant a tree, start a compost bin, or plant a few flowers somewhere. Fairies appreciate the thought, but judge us by our actions.

Some psychics have a natural resonance with these beings and can easily and naturally connect with the fae. I think of this human/fae alliance as being very important right now. Many healers and psychics are connected to the denizens of the fairy world as we humans try to correct our relationship with the natural world.

Recently I worked with Margot, a young woman who is an empath, an artist, and deeply connected to the earth. Margot works as a gardener for a nursery and landscaping company, so she spends a lot of time in the greenhouses and gardens. She has been fascinated by fairies since she was a child and seems rather fae to me herself. She is petite and rather ephemeral, and she loves plants and animals with her whole heart, but isn't totally sure how she feels about people. She is passionate about helping people reconnect to nature through gardening and growing their own vegetables, and in her spare time, she creates urban gardens, helping bring the love of green things to people in cities.

Margot came for a session since she was worried that her house was haunted. There were objects that disappeared one day and reappeared somewhere else later, and her cat would stare and hiss at something in the corner. Fairies and cats seem to have a natural antagonism toward each other. When I tuned in to the disturbances in her house, I didn't see a haunting, but rather a plethora of fairies and earth spirits trying to play with her and catch her attention. They wanted her to know they were there. She created a spot in her garden with a little fairy house and planted a lot of flowers that support bees and other pollinators. The fairies were thrilled with the attention and acknowledgment. They loved the fairy house, not because they can actually live there, but because they admire and appreciate creativity, art, and whimsy.

Sadly, we have become so disconnected from nature that we are in danger of losing our beloved planet or at least irrevocably changing it. Connecting to the fairy realm can help us mend our connection to the natural world and remind us that we are meant to live in harmony with nature.

Tips for Connecting with the Fae

❀ Ask respectfully and politely that they make themselves known to you—and then be grateful when they do. They respond well to whimsy, humor, and humility. They hate arrogance, cruelty, and the assumption that humans are the most intelligent and dominant species on the planet.

- ❋ Get outside in nature, since this is where the fairies are. Set your intention to connect with them. You might say out loud: "Fairies, please listen to me. I want to communicate. So shall it be." They appreciate a good rhyme!

- ❋ Try singing or playing an instrument when you are out in nature; they love music.

- ❋ Fairies inhabit the edges of things, so it's easier to perceive them at dawn and dusk, and at the changes of the seasons. Look to the edge of the fields and the woods or the water and the land.

- ❋ Bring an offering to them: they love music, sweet things, and shiny things.

- ❋ Plant a garden, or bring some plants into your home. If you a have a garden, leave some offerings there too. Plan your garden to encourage and support your local wildlife, so maybe include a water feature, lots of flowers for pollinators, and eschew pesticides, herbicides, and other toxic chemicals.

- ❋ Most fairies will have an automatic connection with gardeners, especially if you leave a little organic whimsy and wildness in your garden. A manicured, pesticide- and herbicide-laden garden will upset them more than attract them.

- ❋ All the fae have a hatred and repulsion to iron. If you create a fairy garden, make sure you don't have iron in your decorations, like iron nails and horseshoes; in fact, the horseshoe at the front door for luck was meant to repel the fae.

- ❋ Get a deck of fairy cards so they can speak directly to you, and be prepared for some fun, whimsy, and maybe a little mischief if you do!

Fairies love a clean house too, which is why they reportedly clean people's houses for them, at least in fairy tales. Be prepared for a little wild magic to happen after you connect with them.

The Spirits of Trees

I find trees to be an easy and rewarding place to start connecting with the nature spirits, since even city dwellers can find a tree to meditate with. Trees are remarkable in that they have both an individual consciousness as well as a collective consciousness. They are connected to each other through their root system and the network of the mycelium, the fungus that grows underground and connects the root systems of plants.

We can easily learn to connect to the spirit of individual trees too, and each type of tree can bring its own specific energy to us, much like a power animal can. You can find books and other resources about what each tree means. For example, cherry trees are strongly connected with love and romance. Their beautiful and fragrant flowers are likened to a love affair—sweet, intense, and perhaps short lived. They bloom for such a short time and their flowers are so gorgeous that it's a reminder to treasure every moment that we are alive, so they help us to be mindful.

We know that oak trees represent strength because they are very long lived, sturdy, and their wood is prized for strength and durability. Willow trees, on the other hand, can help us to remember to be flexible, since they bend in the wind but hardly ever break. Pine trees have a healing energy, and pine resin is wonderful at dispelling sadness and grief. Sit with a pine tree if you are feeling sad or overly emotional, and you will notice that your emotions come into harmony and your sadness eases.

As I mentioned above, you can easily look up all the spiritual and magical associations with trees, just like you look up the power animals. Or try a book like *The Magic of Trees: A Guide to Their Sacred Wisdom & Metaphysical Properties*[14] by Tess Whitehurst. Here is an easy and fun way to start your psychic connection with trees.

Exercise: Creating a Psychic Connection with Trees

You can try this with any kind of tree. It's also fun to identify what kind of tree it is and learn about its medicine.

1. Find a tree that you can sit against. You don't have to be touching the tree, but it's much easier to do this exercise if you are. If you can, sit at the foot of the tree and put your back up against the trunk.

2. It's always polite to ask the tree's permission before you do this meditation. You can ask something like "Can I connect with you?" and see if you feel, sense, or know an answer. Use your pendulum for a yes/no, if you are not sure.

3. You can have a question in mind that you "ask" the tree, much like you would a spirit guide. Or you can just connect and see what happens.

4. Begin by sending your own energetic roots down with the roots of the tree. This is a great way to get grounded yourself.

5. Then feel your crown energy center going up to meet the crown of the tree.

6. Open yourself up, and see if you can feel the pulse of the tree. It will have its own pulse, like a heartbeat, as the sap and the energy of the tree moves up and down the trunk of the tree.

7. Set yourself in an open and receptive state, the alpha state. Open up your psychic sense to observe what you sense, know, feel in your body, or see.

8. Try asking a question or saying hello. You may well perceive an answer.

Write down your experience in your psychic journal. If this is fun for you, try it with many different types of trees. Most likely you will find at least one that feels like it's your type of tree.

The Elementals

While fairies are spirits of individual plants, there are also other spirits of nature. I love connecting with the *elementals*—the spirits of earth, fire, air, and water. The elementals have long been summoned by shamans and practitioners of other earth-based spiritual practices. When we honor these beings and align ourselves to them, we can access their energy for assistance and healing, since they also have their own medicine.

Most of us have one or two of the elements that we easily relate to. The others are something that we need but may not possess.

*   **Air** represents thought, creativity, and the power of words. It is associated with the direction of east. Someone who masters this element is thoughtful,

intelligent, quick witted, and is always able to find the right words. We call someone that has too much of this element an "airhead" or "airy-fairy."

- **Earth** is grounded, stable, and wise. It corresponds to the direction of north and brings the ability to be grounded. Earth people love rocks, crystals, and gardening, and can easily attract wealth and material goods into their lives. If we have too much of this element, we are too earth-bound, to the point of being stagnant.

- **Water** is the element of emotions and is associated with the west. It brings healing, cleansing, deep emotional intelligence, and intuition to people who resonate with water. Water people are natural healers, but too much water can make you a "wet blanket" or put you at the mercy of your emotions.

- **Fire** is the element of transformation, action, and purification. When we burn something, it literally changes form. Fire people are passionate, action oriented, and unafraid of change. However, get too close to the fire and you will get burned, and you might be hot tempered and impulsive to your own detriment.

PSYCHIC TIP: *Connecting with the Elementals*

Contemplate these elements to see if you can discover which two you feel the most aligned with. These are your strengths. You may lack the other two, but if you consciously add them into your life, they will bring you balance. If you have too much earth and water but lack fire and air, for example, light candles or sit next to a bonfire. Incense and wind chimes can bring you the energy of air. Write your observations about your relationship to the elements in your journal and see what you need to do to bring balance to your life.

The air elementals are called *sylphs*, and air is the element of thoughts and words and the power of our creative imagination. Sylphs ride on the currents of air and look a bit like what we think fairies ought to look like—slim, beautiful, and winged. When I am writing and I feel like I need help, I might go stand somewhere in the wind or do other things to invoke both the energy of this element and the spiritual beings that go with it. We can invoke them by lighting incense or ringing a bell—and they love wind chimes, since that is music made by air.

Earth is the element of wisdom and grounding. It is very helpful to work with this element when we need to be grounded. We naturally do this when we spend time with our feet and hands in the soil. Rocks and crystals are part of this element, and so it's very helpful to hold a rock or keep a crystal in your pocket if you need more grounding.

Gnomes are the elemental beings associated with earth, and they can vary in size from small, like the garden statues that we put in our gardens, to really big. I remember once sitting by a waterfall and staring at a huge rock formation. Just for a second my vision altered, and I was sure I could see the shape of a big rock troll reclining there in the sun. I could have sworn that it winked and nodded its knobby head just for a moment, when suddenly my vision shifted again and it was just a big pile of rocks. It is important to remember that these beings exist in a dimension just slightly to the side of our own, and there are times and places when there is a little crossover between dimensions.

The water element corresponds to our emotions, subconscious, and our psychic self. Being in or by the water can help us access our emotions and also help us let them go. Water also has a cleansing aspect to it and brings a peaceful state of being to us. The water elementals are called *undines*. They look like mermaids, and they are present in any body of water. When we need to be soothed, or to touch into our feelings, or to spark our intuition, we can sit next to the ocean or a lake and ask for help connecting inward.

The element of fire is all about change, movement, and purification; it is the element of transformation. When you burn something, it is no longer what it was. The elementals of fire are called salamanders, and they do look like little lizards made of fire. I think that they are the easiest to perceive, and if you stare long enough at a fire, you might see something moving at the base of the flame. When we need to make a change and move forward in life, it's good to invoke this element.

The world of the fae is vast and too much to handle in the short amount of time that we have together in this book. I hope, however, that this helps you understand the basics of this fascinating realm and how to move through it with peace and joy. If you want to connect more to nature spirits, plant something, grow something, or at least spend some time out in nature, and you will reap the benefits of that connection.

What's Next?

Next up, we continue our exploration of the middle realm by talking about what happens when you die. We'll also consider why some people get stuck in the process and become ghosts.

Chapter 9

Deal with and Assist the Dead

I grew up in a rather haunted old Victorian house, and throughout my childhood those wayward spirits felt like friendly members of my own family. When I was little, I would wake up in the middle of the night and see the "gray people" hanging around my room. Honestly, because I had strong mediumship abilities, any house that I have lived in has become haunted. Mediums are like ghost magnets, attracting the uneasy spirits of the dead wherever we go.

The ones in my house were lonely, sad, or confused about why they were there. They were lost and trying to find their way home. I was almost never afraid of them, since they were wispy and unsubstantial. Mostly, I felt sorry for them and tried my best to help and comfort them. They seemed to brighten up a little when they had someone to talk to, someone who could listen to and perceive them. Sometimes that was all they needed in order to move on. Other times, they needed someone to break the news to them that they were actually dead, since they didn't always seem to know.

Occasionally, I would witness this moving on, when other beings of light came and opened a portal for them to cross back over into soul world, and they were so happy to go home again. "Soul world" was what I called the place where the peaceful souls abided. Other people called this place "heaven," but even as child, I preferred this nonreligious name for it.

My experiences with ghosts were a far cry from the Hollywood version, which still has evil, frightening spirits of the dead that seem hell-bent, if you will excuse the pun, on tormenting living humans, especially psychics. These days, it's the paranormal, ghost-hunting type of TV shows and horror movies that are dishing out misinformation about ghosts. I admit to watching and enjoying these shows, but as a psychic teacher, I spend a lot of time debunking the information those shows teach us about what ghosts are, how they can impact us living folks, and how to help them move on.

The Evil Dead—Not!

Let's start right off the bat by clearing up some of these misconceptions about the spirits of the dead. Ghost-hunting TV shows and horror movies would have us believe that every dwelling is chock-full of them. Actual ghosts are pretty rare, and sometimes what we think is a haunting is actually something else entirely, like residual energy or another type of spirit.

Horror movie portrayals show us ghosts that are evil, dangerous, and malevolent. However, most ghosts are not out to harm living humans, and since they have no substance here, there is not much they can do to actually harm us. There is nothing demonic about ghosts, and not every ghost is actually a demon in disguise, as they appear to be in horror movies.

The important thing to remember about ghosts is that they are just people who are lost, stuck, and in need of help. It is true that if you were a jerk in life, you might be a jerky ghost. People really are a mixed bag, so the uneasy spirits of the dead are a bit of a mixed bag too. But if we keep thinking about them as people who need help, it's easier to handle them when we do encounter them. To truly understand what a ghost is, we must consider what is supposed to happen when we die, and why some people get stuck, turning them into the earthbound spirits that we call ghosts.

What Makes a Ghost

Although it can be uncomfortable to think and talk about, the truth is that we are all going to die at some point, and it's a perfectly normal process. Metaphysicians say that we die two deaths. The first death is when the body dies: your heart stops beating and your body shuts down. The second death happens when the spiritual and energetic aspect of the person, their soul essence (sometimes called the *etheric body*) that has inhabited the physical body, also leaves this earthly plane. We know a lot about this process from hearing the stories of people who have had near-death experiences.

There is the feeling of floating out of your body, and then moving toward the light until one is rejoined with one's higher self in soul world. Some people talk about moving through a tunnel or a gray area. Essentially, that tunnel or gray area is a transition space that we go through before the etheric self travels through the astral plane on its way back to soul world.

Sometimes a person gets stuck in a part of the astral plane known as the shadowlands, and they don't make it to soul world. Something happens that keeps them from dying the second death, and they become a ghost. It's usually one of the following things:

- dying so quickly and unexpectedly that they don't know that they are dead

- trauma and/or attachment

- loss of free will, especially around their death as in victims of fatal accidents or murder

- fear of what might happen to them after death

It might seem a like a movie trope, but the truth is that many ghosts stick around here because they don't know they are dead, just like in the movie *The Sixth Sense*. It's an odd thought for us living people, because we are so aware of the fact that we are alive. But when people die very suddenly and outside their own general appointed time of death, or when they die violently, it's a shock that creates trauma and an attachment to their life that makes it hard to cross over.

Most of us have a general kind of agreement with our higher selves about when we are going to die. Of course, this is a bit of a moving target that also depends on how we live and the choices we make on a daily basis. Dying at one's appointed time is a peaceful way to go, and we feel this peace when we say things like "It's so sad, but it was just their time to go." Many people do die at their appointed time, but it's a crazy, random, and sometimes violent world, and sometimes people die outside their appointed time.

This can be the random death of being hit by a drunk driver, dropping dead from a heart attack, accidently overdosing, or some other accident. A sudden death, especially a traumatic one, can leave a person confused about what has happened, and if they refuse to accept their new reality, they can get stuck here. This is especially true if their lives were taken from them by someone else. This explains why those who die at the hands of another person sometimes become ghosts.

If someone's death was very traumatic, it creates a heavy, emotional state that needs to be worked through in order for the person to continue their journey to soul world. This state can also be an accumulation of trauma that the person experienced while still living. However, it's most often the shock of a traumatic death that needs to be processed before a person can fully move on.

As a young psychic, I always knew when I was seeing a ghost, because they would sometimes appear with what I called their "dead face." These poor souls are stuck in their death state, unable to process what happened to them. It is difficult for me, especially as a visual psychic, to see that since they look like a real corpse, but compassion for their pain and suffering has outweighed any squeamishness I might feel.

Attachment is another reason that people can become a ghost—we become attached to people, the places we've lived, and to life itself. This might be the soldier who won't leave their post, or the parent that won't leave their children. I am not sure why ghosts frequent restrooms, but I can assure you that they do. Once I was in the ladies room of a big family restaurant, and there was a wispy woman in there, dressed all in black. She proceeded to tell me that her family was having a wake for her in the function room and that she was trying to accept the fact that she was dead. Her attachment to her young children and her grieving husband was so strong that she was choosing to stay behind and was not ready to move on.

The most stubborn ghosts can be the ones that hang on to this world because they fear what might happen to them in the afterlife. It might be that a strong religious belief tells them that once they let go, they are going to hell for eternity, or if they don't believe in any afterlife at all, they worry that they will disappear into nothingness forever.

Ghosts vs. Your Beloved Dead

It's very important to make a distinction between ghosts who are the uneasy dead and the spirits of people who have successfully crossed over. Ghosts are often freaked out, needy spirits of people who are lost and need help. They don't make good spirit guides, and they are not here to help you. In fact, they need help from us in order to complete their transition back to soul world.

I recently heard from one of my psychic students, a young woman named Bethany, who was so fascinated with the paranormal that she began collecting haunted objects in the hope of communicating with her guides. Bethany was operating under the misunderstanding that hauntings were the same thing as connecting with your guides. Your angels, your beloved dead, and other light beings do not "haunt" objects or places. Anything haunted is a dead giveaway, if you will excuse the pun, that either a ghost or a shadow spirit has created a connection with that place or object. This is why we stay away from Ouija boards and other sketchy psychic pursuits, since they generally only attract the uneasy dead or lower astral entities. Hauntings are sad and a problem that needs healing, compassion, and care from us. We should always approach ghosts and hauntings with a healthy mix of compassion, caution, and common sense.

On the other hand, our beloved dead are those that have fully made the transition to soul world, and they often do come back as guides to offer us help, comfort, and good advice. (In chapter 10, we will go deeply into how to connect with our ancestor spirits and our beloved friends and family who are with us as spirit guides.)

When It's Not a Ghost

When we experience paranormal phenomenon, we might automatically assume it's a ghost. Actual ghosts are relatively rare, and oftentimes it's some other type of spirit that we are encountering. Sometimes what we are experiencing is actually residual energy—that is, leftover human emotional and psychic energy that hangs around places where people have lived. This residual energy accumulates over time into a negative psychic miasma that sensitive people can feel. If it's a place where a lot of horrible things have happened, like a battleground, asylum, or jail, the residual energy is palpable. If it's residual energy, then using sage and other space-clearing techniques help considerably.

Psychic Practice: Discernment Protocol

If you think you have a haunting, you can use your pendulum to ask if it's a lingering ghost that needs help or some other kind of spirit. Using the yes/no/I-don't-know movement from your pendulum, you can ask a series of questions to discern what kind of spirit you might be dealing with. Discernment is the psychic skill that we use to tell what kind of spirit we are dealing with, and while we can learn to distinguish these beings from how we perceive them, it's useful to double-check them with the pendulum.

1. Is it human or nonhuman?

2. If it's human, is it a guide or a ghost?

3. Is it male or female? Is it young or old?

4. Does it need help and healing to move on?

5. If it's nonhuman, is it a helpful, neutral, or nonhelpful spirit?

6. What are the intentions of that nonhuman spirit?

7. Will the typical clearing routine help this spirit move on?

Continue asking these questions in a logical way until you have your answer.

Or we might be encountering a nonhuman spirit like a nature spirit or a lower astral entity. Occasionally, people will feel the presence of their spirit guides and jump to the conclusion that it's a ghost when it really might be a helpful spirit. And sometimes new psychics panic when they feel the presence of a helpful guiding spirit. Fortunately, we can use our pendulum to help us figure out what type of spirit might be hanging around.

Communicating with Ghosts

If you have gone through your discernment protocol and you really do have a ghost, you will most likely experience something along these lines:

- You might experience cold spots and other inexplicable temperature changes.

- You may feel you're being watched or there's another presence in the space with you.

- Objects under two pounds (like keys, your glasses, and things like that) may move around. Ghosts sometimes hide things when they want us to look for something.

- You may sense an emotional heaviness like fear, anger, or despair that won't clear from a space.

- Lights, TVs, and other electronic devices turn on and off. Ghosts can manipulate electrical things easier than they can move objects.

These manifestations are a good indicator that you have an actual ghost rather than a different kind of haunting.

Ghosts will sometimes seek out the living to ask for help, and they are drawn to communicate with us psychic types, especially if we have a natural gift of mediumship. They may attempt to communicate with us and to share with us by running their experiences through our open psychic channels. It's like they are saying, "Look what happened to me!" They are attempting to work through their trauma by sharing their experience, which is totally understandable. It's what living people do too, right? When they do communicate with us, it will probably be through our most open psychic channels:

- Physical psychics will feel things in their body, which isn't always pleasant. My friend Max, who is a physical medium, swears he has felt every single way that you can die, since the spirits of the dead share how they felt with him in a very physical way.

- Empaths might feel strong emotions as a ghost will strongly broadcast their emotions in an attempt to share how they feel: "I was soooo scared! And it felt like *this...*" And then we feel that scared too.

- Auditory psychics might hear footsteps, voices murmuring, taps, or knocking.

- It's quite likely that you might smell something too, like smoke, perfume, or cologne.

- Visual psychics might see apparitions, mists, shadows, or movement out of the corners of their eyes.

Whatever you perceive, it's up to you to decide what you want to do about it. It's totally fine to set a boundary and use the spirit-clearing protocol that we learned in chapter 2 to move a spirit along. Just as you don't have to choose to deal with every living person (and their problems) that you encounter, neither do you have to deal with the dead unless you choose to. I often do choose to try and help them, out of compassion and the spirit of community service, and sometimes for my own peace of mind.

I wrote this chapter while staying in a grand old hotel on Cape Cod in Massachusetts. I cleared a spirit from the third floor where my room was, out of a mixed desire to be helpful and kind, and also the need to get a good night's sleep. She was the ghost of a young teenaged girl who had drowned at the beach and was washed out to sea sometime in the 1960s. Like most ghosts, she wasn't sure what had happened or where she was. She was sad, lost, and lonely, still looking for her friends and family, and confused by the changing landscape. Time is an odd, choppy experience for those stuck in the shadowlands, and she explained that sometimes she was on the beach and sometimes she was wandering around an unfamiliar misty place and didn't know where it was.

I stayed grounded and present, with my heart open and my boundary up so she could share her feelings, thoughts, fears, and experiences, just as I do with living clients. She needed to dump out her whole story and I held space for her. This is called *the witnessing,* and it can really help the uneasy dead let go of their attachments and traumas. It helps them to release all of that heaviness. I always say that clearing ghosts is a lot like doing therapy, only they don't observe your office hours or pay your fee.

Once the teenage girl got it all off her chest, so to speak, and she felt heard and acknowledged, I told her as kindly as I could that she was dead and that she had died years ago. When I speak to the dead, the information is coming in on all channels for me, so I feel it, know it, and hear her voice in my head. Also, I was seeing flashes of images and little movies about what she was explaining, and I could see an image in my mind's eye about what she looked like, which was how I knew she had died in the 1960s. I felt very cold and very sad too, which was how she was feeling.

She was very willing to move on, so when I asked for my guides to open up a connection to soul world, she left very easily and was grateful for the help. I could feel intense joy, relief, and gratitude as she let go of this earthly plane and finally made her transition.

Assisting the Uneasy Dead

We can do things to assist the spirits of the dead to find peace. Some techniques require more training than is within the scope of this book, but the general idea is to compassionately explain the situation to them and see if we can offer our help and assistance—or at least set a boundary if the ghost is a nuisance. I really want you to let go of the idea that ghosts are evil beings with whom we need to battle. They are just people, and we can and should treat them with the same compassion and respect that we treat all people.

Here are some things you can do that might actually bring help and healing to a lost soul. You can do all of these things by speaking out loud and using your pendulum as a backup to check in with any of your psychic experiences.

1. Make sure you are grounded and protected before you start. Open up your psychic senses and pay attention to what you perceive.

2. You can speak out loud and introduce yourself: "Hello, my name is Lisa, and I am speaking to anyone here is who is no longer living."

3. Break it to them in a kind manner that they are dead and that they have a choice to leave anytime. Remind them that there is help and healing waiting for them on the other side and that they will be forgiven and able to forgive once they get there. All things can be resolved from soul world, and there is peace there.

4. Sometimes they want to share their experience with you, so this is the time to pay attention to your feeling and other psychic senses. This is called the witnessing, and it's a lot like therapy for ghosts.

5. Ask your guides and angels to bring in the light. I see this as a big beam of light that appears in the room. Invite any earthbound spirits to step into the light.

6. Call on divine help to assist these spirits to cross over: "In the name of (deity of your choice), I ask that any lost spirit here receive the help and healing they need to find their way home."

7. If they really don't want to leave, and sometimes they won't, ask them to be respectful of the living and to share space in a thoughtful manner. It's not possible or kind to force a ghost to move on, as we still have free will, even when we are dead.

Most of the time, this technique works. If it doesn't, it might be time to call in a professional medium or someone that specializes in removing spirits. There is nothing more stubborn than a stuck ghost who doesn't want to leave. Sometimes we can agree to coexist, if we set some good boundaries.

Maddie bought a condo in what was once the old stone jail right on the waterfront in Providence. That place was haunted to the rafters, and she cleared much of the unpleasant residual energy using sage and some of the other space-clearing techniques that we learned in chapter 2. This lightened up the gloomy energy of the place considerably. There were quite a few ghosts hanging around, and she moved some of them on herself using the technique that we just learned.

However, two very stubborn spirits would not leave. One was the ghost of a prisoner who was murdered and died in the cells, close to what was now Maddie's bathroom. And there was another spirit, that of a guard who was still doing his duty. Maddie called this one the Night Watchman.

Maddie called in a professional psychic medium who is also a feng shui practitioner to perform a house blessing to help remove the spirit of the prisoner. He was afraid he was going straight to hell for his crimes, but eventually he did make the decision to let go and was fully released from this dimension and Maddie's bathroom.

Maddie made a deal with the Night Watchman that if he respected her space, kept to himself, and did not bother her, she would not bother him. They continue to coexist in relative harmony to this day. She knows when she hears the footsteps walking down the hallway outside her front door in the middle of the night that he is walking his rounds and checking in on her. At this point, she says it's a comforting presence to her rather than a frightening one.

What's Next?

I hope that you now understand what a ghost is, how to recognize one, and what to do if you choose to help them move on. Now let's journey to soul world and learn how to connect and communicate with our ancestor spirits and our soul family.

Chapter 10

Receive Support from Ancestor and Soul Family Guides

Welcome to the upper realm! This is the part of the psychic worlds that most people associate with psychic experiences, and it is truly beautiful and awe inspiring. As far as I can tell, it has an infinite number of layers to it, and a vast array of beings that occupy it.

Each layer of the upper realm becomes a little lighter and has a higher vibration as we travel upward to the divine source. The upper reaches of this realm are where the angels and also the ascended masters, prophets, and saints exist. If we go up higher, we encounter the divine beings that we experience as the gods and goddesses as well as the different beings of pure consciousness that populate the cosmos.

In the last chapter, we talked about what happens when someone doesn't make it across to soul world and gets stuck as a ghost. In this chapter, we will focus on the people who have successfully crossed over into soul world, which is a place that most people call heaven. I like the term "soul world" since it doesn't have some of the religious connotations that the word "heaven" has.

It's so incredibly comforting and reassuring to be able to connect with our beloved dead. So, let's zero in on what happens in soul world and the guides that we meet there, which are our fellow humans when they are not actually incarnated on planet Earth.

Soul World

Much has been written and reported about "heaven" from theologians as well as psychics, mystics, metaphysicians, and people who have had near-death experiences, so we actually have a lot of information about it. When we distill all this information down to the commonalities, we can come up with some theories as to what it is like when we finally do make it to soul world. Although we may not truly know until we get there ourselves, this is a good time to let go of our idea of the pearly gates and people sitting on clouds and strumming harps.

What's It Like in Soul World?

Here are some of the common experiences across many traditions about what it's like in soul world. I invite you to run these ideas through your own beliefs and see what feels true to you.

- ✸ There are multiple levels of soul world that we can inhabit when we are there, and where we go depends on our beliefs, expectations, and needs.

- ✸ When we are incarnated, only a percentage of our soul essence is in our body and the rest stays up in soul world to monitor it all. This is our *higher self,* and it constantly sends us suggestions and course corrections through our intuition.

- ✸ When we pass away and reach soul world, we are always met by a team of helpers to assist us processing what happened when we were alive. This is called the *life review.*

- ✸ We reconnect with our soul family, and keep learning and growing while we are there. Some souls choose to work helping others, and other souls opt to heal, rest, or continue to learn.

- ✸ We don't experience time and physicality like we do on earth. However, what we do experience there is a reflection of what we loved about earth.

- ✸ While there is definitely a "heaven," there is no such place as hell where human souls that have committed sins are sent to be punished. In fact, our experiences on earth are more like research experiments, and soul world is where we process and integrate those experiences.

From all that I have learned about soul world, we have nothing to fear about being there. There also seems to be common agreement that residing in soul world is far easier than being alive. Once you get there, come back, visit me, and tell me all about it!

Ancestor Guides

When Annie was a teenager, she woke up suddenly out of a sound sleep to see the figure of a man standing at the foot of her bed. It was her beloved Grandpa Joe, who was more like a father to her, since her own father was mostly absent.

Grandpa Joe sat at the edge of her bed, and they had a long conversation about life and some important decisions that Annie needed to make. He helped her work through some difficulties that she was having. He told her that tough times were ahead and that she would be asked to step up and help her mom more. He was sad and sorry that she needed to grow up so fast, and then suddenly, he was gone. Annie went back to sleep, thinking all the while that Grandpa Joe had come for a visit in the middle of the night. She couldn't quite believe it when her mom told her the next day that he had passed suddenly in the middle of the night, a few states away.

Annie had experienced the most common psychic experience there is, the death-bed visitation. Grandpa Joe had come to say good-bye and give his love and encouragement to Annie for the difficulties that lay ahead. Annie told me that from then on, whenever she was in a pickle, he would show up in her dreams with the same kind of encouragement and practical advice.

Our *ancestor guides* are people who loved and cared for us as family and who have passed over and watch over us from soul world. They can range from our immediate family members to those from generations ago, those we never knew while they were living.

Some people are very connected to their ancestors, while other people don't have much connection at all. Many cultures prioritize honoring ancestors' spirits, and this is a deeply embedded part of their day-to-day spirituality. You might come from a culture that prioritizes honoring your ancestors, or you might have a very close-knit family with strong intergenerational connections. I can tell when someone has a strong connection with their ancestor guides because I see a line of people standing behind them.

Other people don't have a strong soul bond with their biological family, and report that it's like growing up with a group of strangers. In these cases, ancestor guides are not usually a prevalent part of the team of spirit guides. These folks might have a stronger connection to their soul family than their biological family. We will explore soul family a little later in this chapter.

For many of us, especially when we begin psychic work, ancestor guides are often the easiest ones for us connect to. They are so familiar and comforting, and it seems a little more normal and slightly less exotic to have a beloved relative hanging around, even after they have passed away.

Annie continued to feel the presence of Grandpa Joe throughout her life, and he always showed up for her right when she needed him the most. She felt his presence strongly. He came to visit her in a dream on her wedding day and also when her children were born. He loved attending the holidays, when everyone was gathered together, since many of Annie's relatives would talk about feeling his presence, smelling his cologne, or dreaming about him. Grandpa Joe was a loving presence for all and a great example of how our ancestor guides continue to watch over us from soul world.

If you want to connect to someone from your family who has passed over, try this exercise. Of course, it also works for friends and anyone that we were close to in life.

Exercise: Connecting with Our Beloved Dead

This technique can be used to connect to our ancestor guides or anyone that we loved who is now on the other side.

1. Find a picture of whomever it is you want to connect to and light a little white candle in front of it. Tealight candles work very well. You can also use sage or light a stick of incense.

2. Do your basic grounding, clearing, and protecting meditation.

3. When you are ready to begin, say out loud the name of the person you wish to connect with. This acts as an invocation and draws their presence to you.

4. Write down any questions you might have for your ancestor in your journal. Relax and let yourself receive any impressions.

5. Write down what you think they would say in response. If you really let go and don't censor your answers, chances are good you will receive messages from them.

6. This can be like a written question-and-answer session. You write the question down, pause to sense the answer, and then write that down too.

7. Check with your pendulum after you are done to see if what you wrote was a real message from your ancestor spirits.

This technique works very well for people who have a strong auditory psychic sense, and this exercise will also do wonders to strengthen your auditory psychic sense. Practice this technique often to build your confidence in your auditory psychic skills.

One thing to remember is that there is only so much that our ancestor guides can do for us from the other side. They can't interfere with our free will or radically change what's happening with us. They do show up to provide support, love, messages, clues, and hints for us. I sometimes see them as a crowd of loving beings who cheer us on from the sidelines. But like with any other guide, they can't interfere with our lessons and learning.

Not everyone has such a loving connection to their family members as Annie and Grandpa Joe did. When I do mediumship sessions and I feel a relative coming through, I always ask my client if they actually want to connect with them. I don't assume that someone wants to speak to their family member, and we all have the right choose to set a boundary and say no to receiving a message from the other side. I teach my psychic students that, as mediums, our commitment is to honor the needs of the living as much as, if not more than, those who have passed on.

My client Leslie had a difficult and fraught relationship with her mother, Madge, who was both abusive and neglectful. Madge was a new soul and hadn't yet learned to take responsibility for her behaviors. Even once she was dead and in soul world, she had trouble respecting Leslie's boundaries. She desperately wanted to connect with Leslie, and when we did sessions, it felt like Madge was trying to barge in and override Leslie's boundaries. She wanted Leslie to forgive her, and although this was something Leslie was working on, part of her healing required that she set strong boundaries with her mother, even from the other side.

Overall, there is the possibility for tremendous healing from communicating with our loved ones on the other side. When someone dies very suddenly and unexpectedly, there may not have been opportunities to say good-bye or clear up everything that needs to be tended to beforehand. Great healing can happen when a medium facilitates communication between two people who could not find closure. It's so painful for people who are holding on to unspoken feelings, regrets, and grief, and there is amazing relief when we can have those last conversations with our loved ones, even when they are on the other side. Try this on your own and see what happens.

Our beloved dead can always hear us when we speak to them out loud. Say their name out loud and ask them to be present. Say what you want to say, and then see if there are signs, omens, or synchronicities that follow this.

Our loved ones in soul world do hear us when we speak to them, especially when we speak out loud, and they will send us signs that they have heard our messages. This is a wonderful confirmation that we have connected with them; if we are open to seeing the messages, they are all around us. Our ancestor guides often have sweet, poignant, and whimsical ways to let us know that the connection is real. Many people find that birds, butterflies, and dragonflies are a sign that a loved one is present. My friend Maria, for example, would have dragonflies land on her hand on a daily basis, and she knew it was a message from her son who passed away as a child.

Grandpa Joe would send Annie signs through music, since they both loved musicals. They used to sing show tunes together, and he took her many times to see musicals on Broadway. Annie told me this: "I could walk into a store and there would be an obscure song from a musical playing in that store. If I asked him a question and then set my car radio on scan, it would come up with a song from a musical that has the answer that I am looking for."

My psychic student Jaxson said his mother would help him find things in the house. This happened even after she had passed away.

✳ JAXSON'S STORY   *I lost an important paper once and asked my mom to help me find it. I searched the house top to bottom and then suddenly it appeared on the floor of my office. I knew it was her, but I never could figure out where it came from. She also flickers the lights in my room if I stay up too late, and I know that she is reminding me that it is time for bed. She died when I was a teenager, and I miss being mothered like that.*

In many cultures, people create little shrines and altars to honor and remember their ancestors. If you feel like you want to increase your connection to your ancestors, try setting up an altar for them. You might put pictures and objects that belonged to them there, and maybe fresh flowers, candles, and incense. Spend some time meditating at this altar with the intention to connect to your family member or members and see what happens.

I have also seen people greatly increase their psychic connection with their ancestor guides by studying their own genealogy. This is so much easier to do these days with the advent of websites like Ancestry.com.

We don't, however, only have our biological family. We also have our soul family. Although sometimes they overlap, our soul family is also a tremendously helpful group of loved ones that very often are part of our spirit-guide team.

Your Soul Family

For some of us, our soul family is dearer to us than our biological family. Our biological family can be fraught with struggles that offer us opportunities to grow spiritually but that are also painful. It's a good thing that we all belong to a soul family, and we spend our lifetimes incarnating with them over and over again and in many different configurations. With each member of your soul family, you might have spent a lifetime being married, or having been siblings or parent and child.

It's important to let go of the idea that we have one single soul mate who is the only possible soul connection that we have. This romantic fantasy version of soul mates is a very limiting idea; the truth is that we need many different types of relationships in order to grow and evolve as humans. At any given time, some of our soul mates are here on the planet with us and some are not. The ones that are still in soul world can connect with us as spirit guides.

Many years ago, I did a psychic reading and energy healing session for a man named Duncan. He was a combat veteran who came in seeking some help for anxiety and depression. He had some very interesting guides that are a fantastic example of his soul family. On his right side, I could perceive a group of soldiers that had passed on fairly recently. They were his brothers in arms, lost recently in a war. They wanted to tell him they were doing well and that they had his back, even from the other side.

At his other shoulder was a group of strong, tattooed, and fierce warriors, some men and some women. They were Vikings of old and were his original warrior tribe. I could sense that he had spent his first few lifetimes in this tribe of Vikings, and they had become his primary soul family. They also had his back. Their message was that they would never have let him come alone into this crazy world, and no matter where he was, they were with him, helping him face whatever he encountered in life.

Duncan told me that as a child, he had been obsessed with Vikings and all things Norse, since it felt like home to him. He felt much comforted by the fact that both bands of warriors were still with him, supporting him.

Sometimes we feel like we are missing or longing for someone that we don't know about or have recurring dreams or fantasies of someone special who is not present with us right now. Mei Li is an only child but had always felt the presence of a boy around her. Her parents were amused by her imaginary friend, but this boy, whom she called Raven, was not something she ever grew out of. As an artist, Mei Li spent a lot of time drawing his face and longing to meet him. She came to me for some Reiki and psychic work when she was in her late twenties, since she felt her strong and inexplicable connection to Raven was preventing her from establishing a romantic relationship with anyone else, and she wanted to understand this connection to her unseen soul mate.

We did a past life reading in which we uncovered that Raven and Mei Li had been forcibly separated by their parents, who decided that their romantic connection was not appropriate since they were not from the same class and culture. They had sworn oaths to each other to find each other again and not be separated.

Raven was determined to fulfill his oaths, even from the other side. When we cleared the past life and released the oaths, Mei Li was able to grieve and let go of him enough to drop her obsession with him as her one and only soul mate. Shortly after that, she met a man that she later married. Mei Li was still able to connect with Raven from time to time, but it became a pleasurable treat and a comfort rather than something that was blocking her happiness.

Our soul family guides are easy to connect to since there is always a part of us that feels deeply connected to them; they feel so familiar because we have such a strong past life connection to them. This means that we intrinsically and unconsciously trust them. For those reasons, they are sometimes the very first spirit guides that we encounter, especially for those people who are a little nervous about the whole concept of guides. Our deep familiarity with them can help us get past that little threshold of fear. Now, try this great exercise to help you connect to your soul family guides.

Exercise: Finding Your Soul Family

1. Begin with centering and grounding, and then journey to your inner sanctuary.

2. Once you are in your inner sanctuary, spend a few minutes opening up your psychic senses by looking around for what you might see, and noticing what you can hear, smell, taste, feel, or know.

3. Set an intention that you meet at least one member of your soul family, and then begin to open up your senses to perceive.

4. Again, notice what you are sensing. You might sense or feel a presence with you.

5. Can you sense a masculine or feminine presence? Is this person young or old? Is there one person or a group?

6. Ask if there is a name and what relationship this person has with you.

7. Ask how they bring information and messages to you, and if there is anything you can do to increase your connection.

8. When you are done, say good-bye and slowly bring yourself back into the room you are in and back into your body. Release any extra energy you have down through your feet and open your eyes.

9. Record it all in your psychic journal and use your pendulum to verify it if you feel you want to.

It's okay if you don't get answers to all these questions. Remember, too, that sometimes the answers come in the form of feelings, symbols, or metaphors. It will get easier with practice.

What's Next?

I hope that this has helped you find connection with your two families, your biological family and your soul family. These spirit guides add a level of richness and love to our team of spirit guides, and they can be a fantastic source of information for you from the other side. Now we will move up and out of soul world as we explore the world of the ascended masters and the angels.

Chapter 11

Feel the Guidance of Ascended Masters and Angels

We are now headed into the next few levels up in the upper realm. It's glorious up there. And I do mean that word literally: as we rise up in frequency and get closer to the divine source, we feel the glory, beauty, harmony, and order that exist in these higher realms.

In this chapter we will explore the two most beautiful, joyful, and useful upper realm guides, the ascended masters and the angels. We will talk about angels last, since it can be difficult for new psychic students to shift their frequency up high enough to meet these beings of light. (The upper realms are very light and high frequency.) It takes the practice, discipline, and confidence that we learn in working our way through the lower and middle realms to build enough psychic muscle to reach the higher realms.

Let's start by learning about the ascended masters. I love these guides, and most of my own guides come from this group of helpers. Their compassion for humanity is legendary, and they are already woven into our daily lives.

The Ascended Masters

One of my friends, who is also a powerful spiritual teacher, advised me once to stick to the masters, prophets, and saints as my source of spiritual guidance. He felt that they were the best choice for any fellow mystic whose goal is to reach enlightenment and find their way back to the divine, as quickly as possible. He said their role was to forge the road for us and that we can advance more quickly on our spiritual path when we walk in their footsteps.

The *ascended masters* are people who have lived many human lifetimes and have reached enlightenment, and therefore they have completed their cycle of incarnating here on earth. They choose to stay around in order to assist the rest of us humans in reaching that same goal by offering guidance and wisdom, and showing us the pathway back home. We can find that direction through the many sacred texts and mystery schools that they left behind for us.

These ascended masters include spiritual teachers from across the globe—teachers such as Krishna, Lao-Tsu, Mother Mary, Buddha, Jesus, Muhammad, and Kuan-yin. These are some of the better known ones. There are also many that are not famous, well-known, or written about, and I see these amazing but unknown ascended masters assisting people all the time. They can be from any age of humanity and from any place on the globe. Almost everyone has at least one ascended master that works closely with them, and they frequently fill the role of the spiritual director, whose function is to help us with our own spiritual evolution. A critical part of this spiritual evolution is learning self-mastery, in which we learn to come out of our unconscious, reactive states of being and learn how to consciously choose and manage our thoughts, feelings, and actions.

When I was a teenager, I had a running conversation with St. Francis. That confused my hippy, Unitarian parents, since I didn't have a classical education in the Christian religion and, in fact, I never read the Bible until I was in college and studying comparative religion. I have also loved connecting with Mary Magdalen and John the Baptist, as well as Lao-Tsu and a monk from Tibet who called himself Master Sun. He was one of my very first spirit guides, and his presence came with many memories of a lifetime in Tibet where I was taken into a monastery as a young orphan and trained to be a monk and a martial artist.

To this day, Master Sun is one of my primary guides and my spiritual director. He is infinitely patient, kind, and compassionate for the suffering that I have endured in a long and arduous cycle of incarnation. "Oh my child," he has said to me, "your heart is broken again? I am so proud of you for continuing to risk loving someone. Don't forget that all human relationships end on the earthly plane, but continue forever in soul world. And they are reflections only of the love that the divine has for you." This is the type of compassionate support that Master Sun has expressed to me throughout my life.

When I was a small child, he told me his name was Uncle Sun, and his warm presence gave me much comfort during a, at times, lonely childhood. He has cheered me on through every massive mistake and painful misstep that I have made, which he refers to as "research projects," and has also been there to celebrate the successes. I love him so much and know that the feeling is mutual.

There are many ways to work with the ascended masters, and most of us have at least a few of them that we naturally gravitate to. If we were raised in a religious tradition, we might gravitate toward the saints and prophets of that tradition, or we may just feel drawn to and want to connect with new ones.

I can often tell what kind of religious tradition someone was born into by looking at who is around them. The other day I did a reading for a woman who had a crowd of the Catholic saints around her. Kathleen described herself as a "recovering Catholic," but told me that when she was a child in parochial school, she loved the saints more than anything and was comforted to know that they were still around her.

My client Megumi had an interesting mix of Buddhist and Shinto masters from her childhood of growing up in Japan. She also had a few Hindu deities and ascended masters with her, and that connection felt much newer. It all made sense when Megumi said that she had recently come back from a six-month stay at an ashram in India where she took a yoga teachers' intensive training. While there, she started connecting with some of the many ascended masters and gurus from India.

The ascended masters really shine as guides in their abilities to compassionately relate to the human experiences that we have. They know what it is like to love, to suffer loss, to feel pain, and also to directly experience the trials and triumphs of being human. They remember what the sun feels like on your skin and the beauty, hope, and promise of human love. Unlike some of the other upper realm guides, they can comprehend the passage of time and what it feels like to live in a temporal, physical world, so when they say something might happen "soon," they know what that means to us. Their deepest gifts are the ability to share their journey to enlightenment with us so that we might walk in their footsteps.

PSYCHIC TIP: *Calling in the Ascended Masters*

You probably have an ascended master guide that has been with you for many lifetimes. You can invoke them through prayer and meditation, and they will come to you if you request their presence.

As psychics, we can experience ascended masters in many ways, but the most common forms seem to be both as a person and as a collective state of consciousness. Let me explain what I mean by that. We might deeply connect to an ascended master like Jesus or Yogananda, two of my own very favorites who live deep in my own heart. There was Jesus the man, who lived a life that was much written about and reported on. We can connect to his energy by reading these stories and parables in the Bible or by meditation on the prayers and spiritual practices that he left behind for us.

But in addition to Jesus the man and the prophet, there is also something called the "Christ consciousness," which is a much bigger energy than just Jesus the man. The Christ consciousness is a collective energy of the consciousness of compassion. This has become a much bigger energy than just the man, and when we tune in to the Christ consciousness, we can learn much about how to feel compassion for ourselves and for each other. And sometimes that massive consciousness will still appear as a man, since we need that one-on-one connection to relate to the larger consciousness.

Exercise: Connecting with the Ascended Masters

The ascended masters are wonderfully easy to connect to. Here are some foolproof ways to do it:

1. This meditation is even more powerful when we are in a sacred space. Try a church, synagogue, or temple—or somewhere beautiful out in nature. Any place that feels quiet and powerful to you will do.

2. Start with your grounding, clearing, and protecting meditation.

3. Take some breaths into your heart, because it is through our hearts that we connect to the ascended masters. Concentrate on your heart to receive your answers.

4. You can call on an ascended master that you feel drawn to, or just see who is already there. Try saying the name of this being out loud and ask for their presence. Or if there is a prayer related to them, say that prayer.

5. Try asking a question, if you need the answer to a problem. Or ask, "What do I need to know today?" or "What do I need to do to continue to evolve in all ways?" It's also helpful to request a sign, so watch for signs in the days after your meditation.

6. Relax, breathe deeply, and tune in to all your psychic senses for the answers. Pay attention to what happens in your heart as you tune in. Most

people feel deep love, strong emotions, and a profound heart opening when they are present.

7. Record everything in your psychic journal and look for the signs afterward.

I hope you enjoy working with the ascended masters as much as I do.

Now we will discuss angels, which are often people's favorite type of guide. There are, however, many myths and misconceptions around angels, so let's start by clearing those up.

Angels

Angels are probably the most beloved of all the spirit guides. We love everything about them—so much so that people often use the words "guide" and "guardian angel" as synonyms. Indeed, angels have a goal of helping humanity reach its highest potential. Let's jump right in with some ideas about what angels are and what they aren't.

- Angels are not people who have died and gone to heaven. They are non-human spirits who have never been people.

- They don't look like people with wings and halos, unless we need them to look like that so we can relate to them. They are beings of pure energy and look to me like columns of light. Some people experience them as balls or wheels of energy.

- They are immortal beings whose purpose is to oversee the functions of the universe. Only a very small fraction of them deal with humanity and planet Earth.

- They exist in their own dimension called the "angelic heavens" and form a complex hierarchy. Most of the angels that humans encounter are angels and archangels, the two lowest rungs of the angelic hierarchy.

- Angels are neither male nor female, but they will sometimes seem that way to us, especially if they put on the human-looking appearance.

- Angels don't really have human names and are more likely to give their function or title, but they will pick a name you can relate to, much as they pick a form.

- Almost everyone has at least one angel "assigned" to them, which would be our guardian angel, and many people have a strong connection to at least one of the archangels.

The first time I saw an angel, I was overwhelmed and filled with awe. I have never experienced them as people with wings, but have always seen them as massive, high-energy beings with a lot of power and intensity. When I was a little kid, one night I heard a sound like a train running through my room. I think it literally shook my bed when it came in. It looked like a giant ball of energy with wings and flames and lots of eyeballs. I hid under my covers until it went away. A few nights later it came back looking much more human, but it was still clearly not human. This angel "talked" to me by a method of communication called "thought insertion," meaning fully formed thoughts popped into my head, like a massive spiritual download accompanied by a loud ringing in my ears.

It apologized for overwhelming me, told me that I could call it Seraph, and that it was my guardian angel. I swear this being has saved my life a few times, so I know it really is a guardian. Seraph told me that it was one of the *singers* who sang the notes of the symphony, which is how this being experienced the universe. Angels are all about vibration and harmony, and to me their names sound like vast harmonic chords, which we mostly can't even comprehend, so they use something we can understand for a name. Many people know their angels are around when they feel that deep vibration or hear a ringing in their ears.

I had another powerful experience with angels when I was little. I was in the car with my parents, and we were stuck in a traffic jam. Because of an accident, the highway was closed down to one lane. As we drove past the accident, I saw two people lying on the road with the EMTs working on them. One of the EMTs had a very bright white light that looked like a small tornado behind them. I knew this person was going to live and told my parents so. The other EMT had a black funnel behind them, and I knew that this was the angel of death and that person was going to pass. It was intense, but I knew that both angels were there to help the process for all concerned.

Angels exist in the angelic realm, sometimes also called the angelic heavens, as I mentioned above. According to many different faith traditions, there is a hierarchy of angels there. There are many different wheels and spheres of angels whose function is to support the continuation of the universe. They are the servants of the divine being; they are formless and immortal. I wonder if it is their attention to the structure of the universe that gives them such a love of numbers. If you want to connect to your angels, watch for signs in the form of numbers. Often there are repeating number sequences, like 444 or 11-11, that show that the angels are around us.

The angels that we encounter really love humanity, and they support us by giving us unconditional love, encouragement, and advice. Most of the time, I find them charming, funny, and infinitely powerful. Occasionally, I find them intense, and I still shake in my shoes when they show up that way. I do think that we tend to seriously underestimate the power of these beings, and it's been popular in the New Age community to call on your angels for every little thing, much like you would snap your fingers to summon a waiter.

While it is true that angels are here to serve humanity, it's not in some magical wish-fulfillment way. It's not that they mind finding you a parking space and they will do so gladly, if it bolsters your belief in them. It's more about providing us with enough unconditional love and support so that we can accomplish great things on our own.

Generally, they hold a strong energy that we can connect to. You may, for example, have an angel of healing, or the angel of mercy, compassion, or self-love show up for you when you really need that energy. Those types of angels are called the *virtues*, and we can also invite them in when we need them.

PSYCHIC TIP: *Calling on All Angels*

Angels are very powerful beings, and we need to remember to call on them every day for help and assistance. Since free will is such a powerful law of our dimension, we need to ask every day for help. Also remember that angels can help by showing us the way and sending guidance, but they can't solve our problems for us, since the goal is for us to learn and evolve.

Almost everyone that I have ever done a reading for has at least one angel assisting them. Most people have an angel that is particular to them, sort of like an angelic handler, who is very engaged with our own soul's development and growth; they will often be with us for many of our lifetimes. The higher orders of angels, like the virtues and the archangels, watch over many different people at once and are available to anyone who invokes them. For example, if you feel you need extra psychic protection, you can call on Archangel Michael and he will show up for you to help you in that moment.

While everyone has an angel around them, some people really love the angels and connect with them much more deeply than most people do. Sometimes called "earth angels," these people have tons of angels around them. These folks aren't angels who have incarnated on earth, but they are people who have agreed to help the angels do their work here. Earth angels are very kind, compassionate people, the ones that we might say don't have a mean bone in their bodies. They tend to be empaths and extra sensitive and gentle, and they are often somewhat obsessed with angels. If you are an earth angel, you will be sent on little healing missions by your angels to help other people, and sometimes when you say something, the angel is speaking through you.

Since everyone has angels around them, let's talk about how we can connect to them more easily. The quickest and easiest way to connect to your angels is to get a deck of angel cards. There many beautiful ones to choose from. Pick one that resonates with you and add the deck to your daily card pulls. You can ask a question and then pull a card, or you can just pull one and see what the angels have to say today.

Exercise: Meet Your Angels Meditation

Try this meditation to meet your angels. (You can download an audio recording of this meditation at http://www.newharbinger.com/50744.)

1. Begin with your grounding, clearing, and protecting meditation, and journey to your inner sanctuary.

2. Set your intention to meet your angels, and they might just show up there. Remember to open all your psychic senses and pay attention to all your feelings.

3. Look around your inner sanctuary for a conveyance of some kind. Mine has an elevator, but other people find escalators, flying carpets, or even winged beings that can carry them up. If you have an elevator, get in and press the button marked "Angel World," or ask your conveyance to take you up to angel world.

4. When you get there, ask to be greeted by an angelic guide who can show you around and introduce you to your angels.

5. Ask any questions that you might have, including if there is anything you can do to increase your connection and communication with your angels.

6. When you are done, come back down the elevator. Once you are back in your inner sanctuary, thank your angels, knowing that you can come back anytime and communicate with them.

7. Make sure you really ground after this meditation. Rub your palms together and blow any extra energy out the bottoms of your feet before you come back to your room.

Record anything that happened in your psychic journal, and come back to connect with your angels whenever you want to.

Angels and ascended masters aren't the only beings in the upper realm. It is also where we find the divine beings, beings of pure consciousness, and many other, maybe an infinite variety of light beings. I have explored this realm since I was a child, and I still discover new light beings that I have never seen before. It is an infinite universe, after all. I encourage you to keep exploring more and more of these realms and to use your discernment skills to help you connect to spirit guides that are helpful to you.

Establish Your Daily Psychic Routine

We have learned so much about our psychic ability since we started our journey together. I hope that you now have a much better understanding of what your psychic skills really are and how to incorporate them into your daily life in a way that enriches you.

In this book, you have all the tools that you need to continue to awaken your psychic abilities. Your job now, if you want to keep working at it, is to continue your daily practices. Now is a good time to establish a routine that will help you continue to grow your psychic abilities. Over time, you will find a routine that is just right for you. To start, though, try this routine—it's the one that I follow—and then, if necessary, adjust it so it works perfectly for you. Start with your energy management techniques and do your grounding, clearing, and protecting meditation. Then sit quietly for a few minutes to see what comes to you. Make sure to have your journal, pendulum, and your card decks near you. If emotions feel like they are clouding your psychic awareness, spend a few minutes journaling. I have poured out emotions during this time, and also written such mundane things as my to-do and shopping lists, if I feel that those tasks are distracting me.

You can have a specific question in your mind, or if you don't have something particular on your mind, you might just ask something general like "What do I need to know right now?"

Then soften your mind and make it blank as best as you can (it will get easier with practice). Try the journey to your inner sanctuary and practice sharpening your psychic senses by observing what you sense there today.

Sometimes nothing much happens, except that I feel clearer and calmer. And then other times, a psychic message will come into my awareness. I might see or sense a guide, or it might be a knowing, a feeling, or a sensation in my body. Just try to relax through it and stay curious. Ask yourself, *What do I need to know about this sensation?*

Is there something else for me to know? It can be like a tangled ball of yarn that when we pull on one thread, more follows.

At this point in my life as a psychic, I totally trust that if there is something I need to know, my guides will get that information to me. And if there is nothing there, it's because all is calm at the moment and no news is good news. I trust that if I am being stubbornly resistant about dealing with some aspect of my life, the information that I need will come to me in a dream, even a recurring dream, until I get the message.

I also know that if I am really triggered, my own psychic information dries up until I clear the trigger and work through my emotions. In the meantime, I can use my cards and pendulum to get what I need, or it might be time to call one of my psychic friends and ask someone else to read for me.

It's very exciting for me that even though I have been doing psychic readings for over thirty years, I still learn new things every day. And that is what I want for you too. Thanks so much for coming on this journey with me. I know if you practice what we have learned together in this book, you will reap the benefits of accessing the help, wisdom, and guidance that is available to all of us when we awaken our psychic abilities.

Acknowledgments

So many wonderful people have gone into making this book—I truly never could write a book without help. And by the way, if you're thinking about writing a book yourself, please don't go it alone. It takes a community of supporters, coaches, helpers, and friends, and I sure have some stellar ones.

Deep and sincere thanks to Ogmios Lieberman, who is a brilliant artist and continues to get the illustrations just right, and who also has helped tremendously in encouraging and supporting me along the way.

Thank you to my own support staff, especially to Kelley Twombly, who makes sure that I still show up on time and in the right place, even when I have book deadlines. And to my wonderful coaches Ruble Chandy and Trish Blain, who are both incredibly supportive and also good at aiming the bar higher and higher.

So much love to my family—you are always gracious about the times when I have to disappear for a little while to get everything done. Thanks to my kids—Grayson, Devin, and Genevieve—love you so much! And to my sister, Sara, and her lovely family who invite me over for dinner and a hot tub just to keep my sanity. Thanks so much, Mom, for being so happy and lucky, and to Dad for watching over me and encouraging me from the other side.

Love to my dear friends who are patient and loving, despite missing time together. Michelle, Maura, and Raffaele, bless you!

And to my New Harbinger family, it truly is a collaborative effort. Special thanks to Jess O'Brien, who gently nudges me and reminds me that it's time for another book, and to all the other editorial wizards who had a hand in this book. There is an alchemical magic in the editing process that turns everything from lead to gold.

Thank you to Bill Gladstone for sealing the deal.

And deep and soulful thanks to all my psychic students, especially my apprentices. This one is for you. Thank you all for helping me to fulfill my life purpose as a teacher and a mentor. I want to create an army of healers to go out and save the world, and you all are it. Keep shining and spreading the light.

Xoxo—Lisa

Endnotes

1   Lisa Campion, *Energy Healing for Empaths: How to Protect Yourself from Energy Vampires, Honor Your Boundaries, and Build Healthier Relationships* (Oakland, CA: Revel Press, 2021).

2   Anodea Judith, *Wheels of Life: A User's Guide to the Chakra System* (Woodbury, MN: Llewellyn Publications, 1987), 133.

3   Carl Jung, *Man and His Symbols* (New York: Dell Publishing, 1968).

4   Juan Eduardo Cirlot, A *Dictionary of Symbols: Revised and Expanded Edition* (New York, NY: New York Review Books Classics, 2020), 95.

5   Kelly Sullivan Walden, *It's All in Your Dreams: Five Portals to an Awakened Life* (Newburyport, MA: Conari Press, 2013).

6   Kelly Sullivan Walden, *I Had the Strangest Dream: The Dreamer's Dictionary for the 21st Century* (New York: Grand Central Publishing, 2006).

7   Mystic Michaela, *Your Angel Numbers Book: How to Understand the Messages Your Spirit Guides Are Sending You* (Avon, MA: Adams Media, 2021).

8   Brian Browne Walker, *The I Ching or Book of Changes: A Guide to Life's Turning Points* (1992; repr., New York: St. Martin's Griffin, 2019).

9   Jacob Nordby, *The Creative Cure: How Finding and Freeing Your Inner Artist Can Heal Your Life* (San Antonio, TX: Hierophant Publishing, 2021).

10 Elaine Clayton, *The Way of the Empath: How Compassion, Empathy, and Intuition Can Heal Your World* (Newburyport, MA: Hampton Roads Publishing, 2022).

11 Robert Bruce, *Astral Dynamics: The Complete Book of Out-of-Body Experiences* (Newburyport, MA: Hampton Roads Publishing, 2009), 138.

12 Don José Ruiz, *Shamanic Power Animals: Embracing the Teachings of Our Non-Human Friends* (San Antonio, TX: Hierophant Publishing, 2021).

13 Steven D. Farmer, *Animal Spirit Guides: An Easy-to-Use Handbook for Identifying and Understanding Your Power Animals and Animal Spirit Helpers* (Carlsbad, CA: Hay House, 2006).

14 Tess Whitehurst, *The Magic of Trees: A Guide to Their Sacred Wisdom & Metaphysical Properties* (Woodbury, MN: Llewellyn Publications, 2017).

Lisa Campion is a psychic counselor and Reiki master teacher with more than twenty-five years of experience. She has trained more than one thousand practitioners in the hands-on, energy-healing practice of Reiki, including medical professionals; and has conducted more than fifteen thousand individual sessions in her career. Campion is author of several books, including *The Art of Psychic Reiki*. Based near Providence, RI, she specializes in training emerging psychics, empaths, and healers so they can fully step into their gifts—the world needs all the healers it can get!

Foreword writer **MaryAnn DiMarco** is an internationally recognized psychic medium, author, speaker, healer, and spiritual teacher. She is author of *Medium Mentor* and *Believe, Ask, Act*. To learn more about her abilities, readings, and classes, please visit www.maryanndimarco.com.

MORE BOOKS for the SPIRITUAL SEEKER

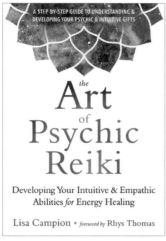

ISBN: 978-1684031214 | US $19.95

ISBN: 978-1684035922 | US $18.95

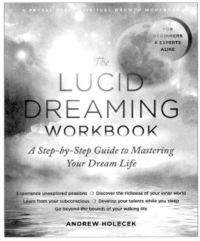

ISBN: 978-1684038909 | US $16.95

ISBN: 978-1684035021 | US $21.95

newharbingerpublications

NON-DUALITY PRESS | REVEAL PRESS

Did you know there are **free tools** you can download for this book?

Free tools are things like **worksheets**, **guided meditation exercises**, and **more** that will help you get the most out of your book.

You can download free tools for this book— whether you bought or borrowed it, in any format, from any source—from the New Harbinger website. All you need is a NewHarbinger.com account. Just use the URL provided in this book to view the free tools that are available for it. Then, click on the "download" button for the free tool you want, and follow the prompts that appear to log in to your NewHarbinger.com account and download the material.

You can also save the free tools for this book to your **Free Tools Library** so you can access them again anytime, just by logging in to your account! Just look for this button on the book's free tools page.

+ Save this to my free tools library

If you need help accessing or downloading free tools, visit **newharbinger.com/faq** or contact us at **customerservice@newharbinger.com.**